DOUGH

Simple Contemporary Bread

DOUGH

Simple Contemporary Bread by Richard Bertinet

with photography by Jean Cazals

Kyle Books

For Jo, Jack, and Tom
With all my love

Acknowledgements

To Sheila Keating, without whom I would not have got over the first hurdle, let alone past the finishing post; Kyle Cathie and her team for believing in this book; Jean Cazals for the amazing pictures, and to Susanna Cook and the team at allies for putting the jigsaw together.

To Tim White and John Warwick for making me a movie star (!); Sue Rowlands for props and croissants, Daniel Hopwood (www.danielhopwood.com), Model Catering (www.modelcatering.com), and Bill Amberg (www.billamberg.com) for letting us borrow their beautiful things, and Amanda at Flirty for trees and flowers.

To John Lister and Clive Mellums at Shipton Mill (enquiries@shiptonmill.com) for their advice and wonderful flour; Dan Lepard (www.danlepard.com) for his support and friendship; and A.J. Tee at the French Croissant Company for his continued understanding.

To Alison, Sophie, and Dan for looking absolutely fabulous and for getting out of bed for nothing; Joe, Alice, Eddie, Charlie, and my boys for being our (guinea) pigs; and to Jane, Karl, and Jackie for accommodating the overflow so graciously.

To Christine for her fabulous summer pudding and marmalade and, together with Penny and Vicky, for proving my point, that baking is fun; and to Kerry and Anna for being great friends and making the world around me run so smoothly while this book has been in the making.

Finally, to The Boss, for being there.

Richard is teaching and cooking at The Bertinet Kitchen in Bath. www.thebertinetkitchen.com

This edition published in 2005 by Kyle Books
An imprint of Kyle Cathie Limited
www.kylecathie.com

Distributed by National Book Network
4501 Frobes Blvd., Suite 200
Lanham, MD 20706
Phone: (301) 459 3366 Fax: (301) 429 5746

Text © 2005 by Richard Bertinet
Photographs © 2005 by Jean Cazals
Book design © 2005 by Kyle Cathie Limited

First published by Kyle Cathie Limited 2005

ISBN:1 904920 20 9

The Library of Congress Cataloging-in-Publication Data is available on file.

Bertinet, Richard.
Dough: Simple Contemprary Bread/Richard Bertinet
1. Cookery, Baking

Copy editor: Sophie Allen
Design: Allies
Indexer: Alex Corrin
Proofreader: Brenda Updegraff
Americaniser: Delora Jones
Production: Sha Huxtable & Alice Holloway
Color reproduction: Colourscan Pty Limited
Printed and bound in Singapore by Star Standard Industries Limited

contents

Companion: someone you share bread with

I have been a baker most of my life and crazy about bread since I was a kid, but it wasn't until I started teaching people how to bake simple breads at home that I really appreciated what fun, and what a sense of achievement almost everyone experiences when they realize, for the first time, what can be done with some flour, yeast, water, and a little salt. Breadmaking doesn't need to be daunting or mysterious and you don't have to be born a baker. Baking is for everyone. The aim of this book is simply to get you hooked on making bread. I'm not going to delve into the chemistry of breadmaking, analyze the properties of different flours, list masses of equipment, or baffle you with complex techniques.

I look at it this way: do you need to know how a carburetor works to learn how to drive a car? No. Well nor do you need to immerse yourself in science to bake a wealth of wonderful breads. All the breads in this book I bake at home for my family and friends in my standard domestic oven, with my two young boys distracting me as much as they can. I teach these recipes to the people who come to my bread classes, and I love the moment when the baking is finished and we all sit down with the breads we have made, some good cheese and ham and a glass of wine, and relax and enjoy the sense of achievement. I find that people really hate to break the spell—and nothing gives me more pleasure than to hear from them that they have baked the breads again successfully at home, and really enjoyed themselves in the process.

There is another reason for writing this book—the current climate of concern about the quality and safety of the food we eat, and the worry about additives, fat, sugar, salt, and obesity. So much of what we eat is produced on a massive scale, with such a long and complicated chain of ingredients, suppliers, and processes that many people are turning to smaller, artisan producers and farmers who can supply them with traceable food produced in simple, traditional ways, which they feel that they can have faith in. And what could be more trustworthy than your own bread, baked by your own hands in your own kitchen, using the best quality ingredients you can find? I will never forget the first time I visited a big industrial bakery in Britain, watching the loaves being mixed in minutes with the help of all kinds of "improvers" and additives, and churned out on a massive scale—it gave me the shock of my life. I had never seen anything like it—it was so alien to everything I knew about bread.

I first fell in love with bread when I was very small. My uncle had a big bakery in Paris, my mother had at one time worked behind a bakery counter, and I was fascinated by the boulangerie in my home town in Brittany. When I was on vacation from school I used to go down there and stand on tip-toes so I could peer over the counter into the bakery itself. I could see the men working in their t-shirts, covered in flour, taking the bread out of the enormous ovens. The warm, yeasty smell was so seductive. When I was 12 or 13 years old I remember being asked in school, "What do you

want to do when you are older?" and I replied that I wanted to be a baker. I had a friend whose uncle had a bakery, and he told me that I could come and work with them early one morning. I stayed with my friend in the house above the bakery, but I couldn't sleep for excitement. By midnight I had crept down—I couldn't keep away.

Baking was in my blood and, as soon as I could, I did my pre-apprenticeship, spending two weeks at school and two weeks and every weekend in the bakery. French bakeries are hard-working places but they have a magic, too. There was a particular moment that I still miss, at around four o'clock in the morning, when the ovens were emptied, and there was no sound, except for the newly baked bread "singing". That's what we used to call the crackling sound that big loaves make when the crust breaks as it cools down—listen for yourself: when you hear it sing, that's when you know you have a good crust. In France of course, most people never bake their own bread because the tradition of buying it fresh, every day, is so strong. There is a bread for every occasion: a ficelle for breakfast, a baguette for lunch, a pain de mie for croque monsieur, a bigger pain de campagne or sourdough to put on the table or to keep and toast through the whole week. In France if there is no bread on the table at a mealtime, it is a major catastrophe.

In Britain I knew there was a strong tradition of home breadmaking, but when I arrived here in 1988, I was shocked to find that very few people were bothering any more, not because there was a fantastic bakery around every corner, but because the staple diet was the sliced white loaf. There are over 200 varieties of bread available in the UK these days and we buy the equivalent of 9 million large loaves every day, but around 80% of the bread we buy is the sliced, wrapped sandwich loaf—and 75% of that bread is white. Most of the commercially made bread is produced using what is known as the Chorleywood Bread Process, invented in 1961 by the British Baking Industries Research Association at Chorleywood. The process is all about producing a cheap loaf, and it uses high–speed industrial mixers which produce the dough in minutes. Because the flour isn't necessarily the highest quality, and because you need to add as much water as possible to make the bread more commercially viable, pre-mixed "improvers" and extra ingredients are added, such as emulsifiers, preservatives, fats, antifungal sprays, and added enzymes, to make the dough softer, "improve" the volume and prolong shelf life. As there is no real tradition of buying

bread daily in Britain, one of the first demands of any mass produced bread is that it will be able to sit on the shelf for up to a week without deteriorating—"fresh?"—that's not my definition of fresh.

Of course there is a place for commercial sliced bread—to take as bait when you go fishing, or to make a bacon sandwich when you've got a hangover! —but if you make your own bread, you needn't

worry about these suspicious ingredients because you are in control—and what do you need? Only flour, yeast, water, and salt. No improvers, no enzymes, no stabilizers, emulsifiers, or preservatives. And once you see the baking process in its natural, pure form then you can start asking questions to the people who make your bread commercially. Why do they need to add the contents of a chemistry set to your loaf? Skilled bakers can make bread on a large scale without bagfuls of additives, provided people are willing to pay a bit more for their bread—but there lie the two big issues: price and skill. Where have all the bakers gone?

Thankfully I think they are reappearing and, as they do, people are beginning to realize that it is worth paying a little more for the beautiful artisan breads they produce. At last there is a real surge of interest and excitement about breadmaking in this country, which is gathering pace. If I flash back to when I first arrived in Britain, I was amazed to find that in restaurants they seemed to serve bread almost as a canapé, before the meal, then it would be taken away, as if it was something separate from the rest of the food. However, over the last 10–15 years, there has been a huge revolution in the way we think about food. And while at first, bread was overlooked in the new wave of excitement about restaurants and cooking, gradually chefs have begun to wake up to the idea that, as soon as someone sits down at the table, the arrival of a selection of breads with different flavors, shapes, and textures immediately creates a welcoming and warm atmosphere and an expectation of more good things to follow. And as Britain's café culture continues to grow, sweet doughs, from croissants to brioche, have come into their own.

Of course what happens in restaurants influences the way we cook at home, and I quickly began to see that there was a real desire to bake, which was only held back by the idea that the process must be too complicated or time consuming; something to do on a special occasion with the kids, maybe, but not on a regular basis. That is when I began my breadmaking courses, teaching baking to a cross-section of people, from absolute beginners to those who had tried to make bread once, ended up with something that resembled a brick, and were so disillusioned they never tried again. I never dreamt that the classes would be so popular or so rewarding. I never get tired of seeing people's faces as their first bread comes out of the oven; they can't believe that they have made it themselves, without buckets of sweat and frustration.

People often say that those who like to bake and those who like to cook are made in different molds. Well having worked both as a baker and a chef, I have never thought of baking and cooking as separate activities —to me baking bread is part of making a meal (it's also the best time to make dough, when the kitchen is warm from cooking) and I can't imagine dinner on the table without bread. Personally, I would love to see more chefs having a go at making their own bread. And every time I eat out, or talk to a chef about a combination of ingredients, I find myself thinking, "I wonder what would be a good bread to go with that?" or, since bread is a natural carrier of flavors, "How would those tastes work in a bread?"

Once you get into the habit of baking regularly, you can always have some bread part-baked in the freezer, ready to be finished off in the oven. Imagine giving your friends freshly baked fougasse, breadsticks, or rolls when they come round to dinner; or the children coming home from school and asking for a chunk of fresh bread. Your bread.

bread talk

What you need

Hands—I always think it must be daunting to pick up a bread book that lists pages of expensive "essential" equipment. The truth is that your hands are your most valuable tools—and really "feeling" the dough is what breadmaking is all about.

Baking stone—in a traditional baker's oven, the bread is slid, using a wooden peel (or paddle), onto the hot brick floor, so that it starts to bake immediately underneath (it's the same principle as getting a grill-pan hot before you put on a steak). At the same time, a steam injection system provides humidity which helps the crust to form. You can come close to creating a similar environment at home by getting a baking stone ready in the oven, and sliding your bread directly onto it. I have a piece of granite which stays in my oven all the time (you don't have to spend a lot of money—mine was an offcut that I found in a reclamation yard, and it's perfect). When I switch on the cooker in the morning the stone is already in there so that by the time I come to bake it is thoroughly hot. Then, when I am ready to go, I just slide the loaves onto it, using a wooden peel or flat baking tray. You can also use a heavy cookie sheet, turned upside down so that it is flat.

Weighing scales—baking relies on exact measurements, so I weigh everything, including liquids, which is more accurate than relying on a level in a measuring cup. In many of the recipes which involve dividing the dough up into small rolls, baguettes, etc., I suggest that you weigh each piece of dough, and try to get them all equal—simply because, if you have lots of different sizes, some will bake quicker than others.

A mixing bowl—big enough to hold 2 or more pounds of dough. Apart from mixing, you also use the bowl for, resting the dough. I use a stainless steel bowl.

Lintfree dishtowels—you only need a handful, for covering dough, and lining trays while the dough rests. I use the same ones over and over again. I keep them in a separate drawer and don't wash them in between breadmaking sessions—the last thing I want is towels smelling of laundry detergent covering the dough. When you have finished making your bread, you just need to shake or brush the towels very well and let them dry. Over time the fabric becomes impregnated with natural yeasts and flavors, and the towels become an organic part of the whole breadmaking process.

Plastic scraper—this cheap little gadget is like an extension of my hand. I use it all the time: the rounded end to mix the dough, to help turn it out from the mixing bowl so that it comes out easily in one piece, without stretching, and to scrape up and lift pieces of dough from the counter. The straight edge can be used for cutting and dividing the dough—it's also fantastic for scraping the ice from your windshield in winter! If you don't have a scraper you can use a large flat wooden spoon or even a sample credit card you receive in the post.

Razor blade—for slashing the tops of loaves and rolls to help create more crusty edges. Of course you can use a sharp knife, but the razor blade fitted into a handle, known as a lame, is the traditional baker's "pen" which you use to put your "signature" on your bread, and it does the job swiftly and cleanly.

Wicker dough-raising basket—not essential at all, just a traditional and lovely thing designed to hold round loaves while they are rising for the second time. The wicker makes an ideal container because it allows the air to circulate around the dough and let it breathe—and you can clean the basket and use it to serve the bread afterwards.

Wooden peel—this is really useful for transferring your raised bread to your baking stone or tray in the oven. If you don't have one, you can use a flat-edged cookie sheet, or if you only have a baking tray with a lip, turn it upside-down. Flour it well.

Water spray—the kind you use for spraying houseplants is perfect for misting the oven with water as you put in bread that needs to develop a good crust and color.

Timer—don't assume you will remember to take the bread out at the right time! I have three timers all on the go, otherwise I know I will get caught out when one of the kids distracts me, or the phone rings.

Soft brush—mine is like a little handbrush you might use for sweeping. I keep it on my work bench for brushing off flour. Don't wash down your bench until the end of your breadmaking session. Just scrape off any pieces of dough with your scraper, brush away any unwanted flour, and then when you are completely finished, you can wash down your surface thoroughly with soap and water.

ingredients

Flour—all I want to say about flour is: use proper, good-quality hard-wheat flour (organic, if possible), and the best quality you can afford. One of the questions I am always asked in my classes, is where do I buy mine from, as once people have made bread successfully, I find that when they get home they want to reproduce everything they have done exactly, using identical ingredients. Well, I buy most of mine from Shipton Mill in Tetbury, Gloucestershire, England, who offer an amazing range of flours from all over the world, for use in every style of baking. Many of the flours are organic, and all of them are stone-ground and untreated.

Yeast—I am tempted to say only use fresh yeast, and avoid dried, but it is worth having some dried yeast in the cupboard for that moment when you have an overwhelming urge to bake, and you find you are out of fresh. One of the things that seems to amaze people is how easy it is to use fresh yeast. I don't believe in adding sugar and warm water to yeast to "activate it" before using it—inevitably I find people add water that is way too hot, which will leave you with a sticky mess, and anyway none of this is necessary. All you need to do is rub the yeast into the flour using your fingers, just as if you are making a crumble. If you do have to resort to dried yeast, treat it in exactly the same way.

Water—I use tap water in all my recipes (at room temperature). If you have a water filter, even better. Frankly I don't see any benefit in using bottled water, which has probably been sitting inside glass for a few years—I like to drink it, yes but, for breadmaking, I wouldn't bother.

Salt—use fine sea salt, preferably organic. I know there is a lot of angst about the salt content in bread these days, yet the absurd thing is that it is often the very people who are worrying who are also giving their children bags of salt-laden potato chips to eat. All I can say is that I happily give my children fresh homemade bread to eat, but they don't have chips or any other processed food full of hidden salt. Salt in bread stabilzes the fermentation and helps the color and flavor. In some parts of the world, like Tuscany, they traditionally eat bread made with no salt, but to me it is like eating a steak that hasn't been seasoned properly. If you want to reduce the level of salt, of course you can, but the results won't be as good.

bread talk

Every baker has his own terms and expressions. These are the ones I use and that you will come across in the book.

Working the dough—the kneading technique that most people are taught in Britain and America is quite different from the one we use in France, which is all about getting air and life into the dough. So, instead of using the word kneading (which sounds too harsh), I prefer to talk about working the dough (page 24).

Resting—this is the time when the worked dough is left, usually for about 1 hour, covered with a lintfree dishtowel, in a warm, draft-free place, during which time it will rise to around double its volume and develop its structure, while the flavor matures. "Where is this warm, draft-free place?" "Warm" is, after all, quite a loose term which might suggest different things to different people. What I mean by warm is the ambient temperature in my kitchen after I have had the oven on since early morning (around 77–86°F). You can use a microwave (turned off, of course), or a kitchen cupboard, but I would avoid using the top of your stove, which will be too hot and will dry out the dough. If you do feel that your dough is drying out as it rests, move it away from any obvious heat source and spray some water onto the top of the towel that covers it.

Second rising—this is the time when the dough is left again, after it has been molded, or shaped into loaves, rolls, etc. Again it will expand to around just under double its volume—this will usually take around 1 hour. The reason I say "just under" double is that, until you get a feel for baking, it isn't always easy to guage that moment when the volume of your dough has doubled, and you will get better results if you slightly under-rise your bread, than if you over-rise it.

Folding—usually in America, I find people are taught to "punch down" the dough to take the air out of it once it has rested. I hate that term, because it suggests you need to bash the dough to bits, whereas you need to be much more gentle with it. I just turn the dough upside-down, then fold the outside edges of dough in on themselves a few times, pressing down each time, and turning the dough around. Folding and pressing down the dough is also the technique I use to mold the dough into different shapes.

Baking—it may sound obvious, but bread is "baked" not "cooked". I often hear people talking about "cooking" bread, which to me is as weird as hearing someone saying they're going to "bake" a piece of steak.

Ferment—some bakers use the term "levain", which means the same thing—a piece of dough that has been left at least 4–6 hours to "ferment" and which adds character, flavor, and lightens the finished bread. A few of the breads use a "poolish", which is just the name for a particular style of ferment.

working the dough

second rising

ferment

proving

folding

baking

Color Chart—when you start baking and read things like "bake until golden brown" it doesn't necessarily mean that much—so I thought I would help by giving you a color chart, showing the various shades the crust will go through as you continue to bake.

Note: Of course this only really applies to white bread, as brown, or rye bread will necessarily be darker.

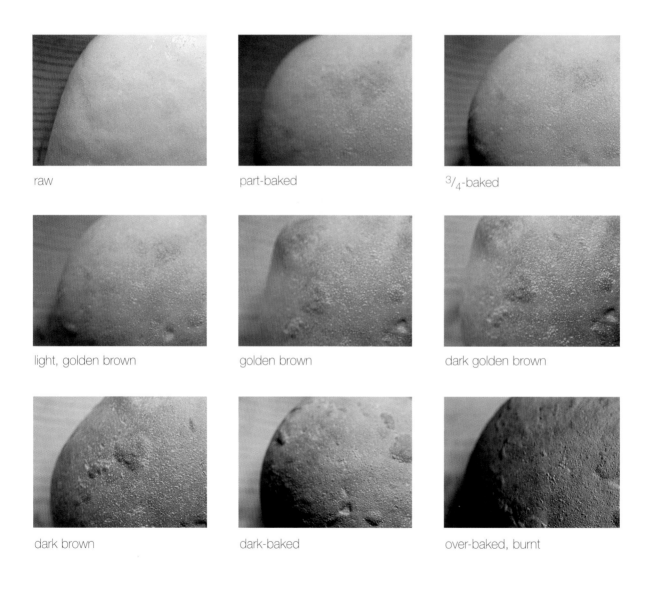

raw   part-baked $^3/_4$-baked

light, golden brown   golden brown   dark golden brown

dark brown   dark-baked   over-baked, burnt

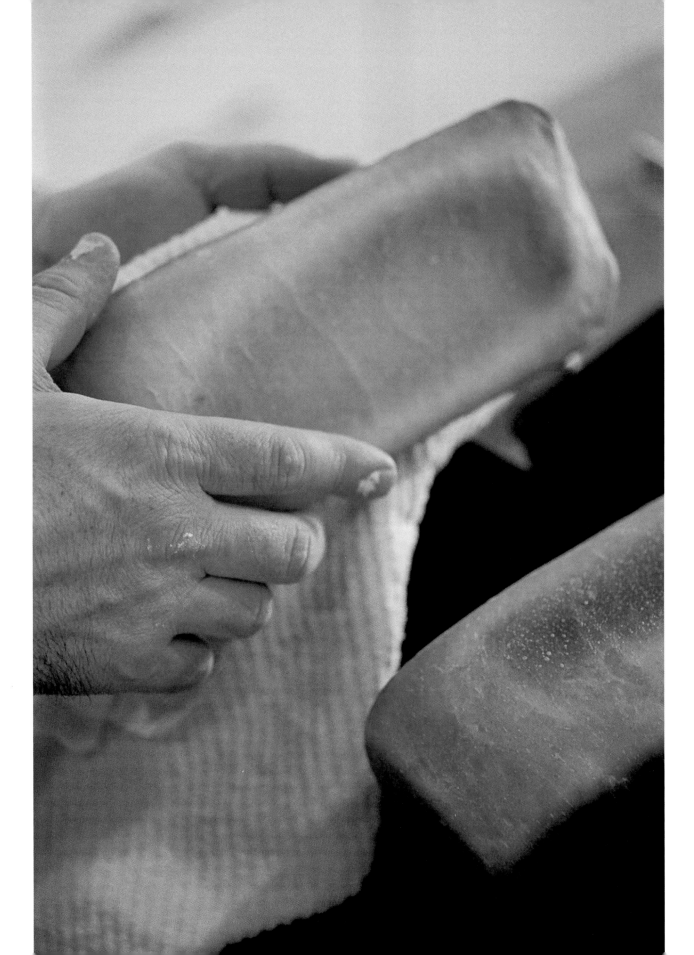

shop-bought loaf typically contains

Wheatflour, water, yeast, wheat protein, salt, vinegar, dextrose, soya flour, vegetable fat, emulsifier E472e (mono- and diacetyle tartaric acid esters of mono- and diglycerides of fatty acids), flour treatment agent E300 (absorbic acid), preservative calcium propionate (to inhibit mould growth)

**homemade
loaf
contains**

flour,
yeast,
salt,
water

the dough

Each of the chapters that follow begins with a slightly different dough recipe and, from this "parent" dough you can bake a vast variety of styles of bread really easily. The beauty of it is that it takes no time at all to fill a bread board with, say, striking-looking fougasses, breadsticks, Moroccan rolls (from the White Dough chapter), or poppy seed stars, sesame plaits and chunks of pecan and cranberry, or cardamom and prune bread (from the Brown Dough chapter), and no one will guess that they are all part of the same "family". Just to keep things interesting, I have finished all but the Sweet Dough chapter with a slightly more challenging bread for you to try once you begin to feel comfortable with baking. Though the doughs vary, the technique for making each one is identical.

To prepare

• Whenever you bake, your very first job is to preheat your oven to its highest temperature (475°F if possible—except for the breads in the Sweet Dough chapter, when you should start off at 425°F) and put your baking stone or heavy baking tray (page 10) into the oven. Do this as early as you can, so that not only the oven, but the whole kitchen warms up—you'll find the dough is more responsive in a warm atmosphere. For some of the recipes you will need to turn the oven down to a lower temperature, just before you put the bread into the oven.

• If you have an accurate scale, weigh all the ingredients carefully—I even weigh my water, as it is much more precise than trying to judge volume at eye level. You can see for yourself by measuring 13 fluid ounces of water in a measuring cup, then weighing it. Do it a few times and I bet that every time there will be a slight variation in the weight. In most cooking this would be neither here nor there, but in baking it is important to be accurate about your quantities.

• In some of the recipes for flavored bread you will need to incorporate extra ingredients—fruit, nuts, spices—at the end of working the dough by hand or mixing in a mixer, so check with the recipe you want to make before starting to make the dough. Having made your own wonderful wholesome bread, make sure that when you flavor it you do it justice, by adding really good-quality ingredients.

For the freezer: All of the breads in this book can be frozen, except for the Puff Ball. However, I would recommend you part-bake them first to retain freshness. Make sure the bread is thoroughly cool before freezing, wrap in wax or parchment paper and seal in a plastic food bag. To use the bread, put into a cold oven, turned to 400°F—by the time the oven reaches the temperature (about 12–15 minutes) the loaves should be baked. If you are already using your oven then just reduce the baking time to about 8–10 minutes. (Keep an eye on smaller breads that may take less time.) As an exception, breads made from sweet dough should always be fully baked before freezing. Defrost them fully at room temperature then reheat in a low oven (350°F) before serving.

make the dough

• Rub the yeast into the flour using your fingertips as if making a crumble, until it disappears into the flour. Add the salt and then the water. Hold the bowl with one hand and mix the ingredients around with the other (or use the rounded end of your scraper) for 2–3 minutes until the dough starts to form.

• With the help of the rounded end of your scraper, turn the dough out onto the counter. Even though the dough will feel quite soft and moist (and look like thick, sticky porridge) do not add any flour to the counter.

add the water

mix the ingredients

turn out the dough

don't flour the surface

People are always amazed when I tell them that I work the dough by hand without flouring the counter. Sometimes when I am giving breadmaking classes, to prove the point that you don't need any flour, I put some extra water into the dough, to make it really sticky. No one believes that it will really come together without flour, yet it does, simply by working it, stretching and folding, to trap the air inside. Think about it: if you continue adding flour at this stage—before you know it you can easily put another 3/4 cup into your dough, which will firm it up and change its make-up—then you are far more likely to end up with a "brick". If you work the dough without flour, it allows you to keep the dough softer, so the finished bread is lighter, more airy and exciting.

work the dough

• Begin to work the dough. The idea is to stretch it and get as much air into it as possible. Forget the way you have probably been taught to knead the dough, by pummeling it with the heel of your hands and rotating it. The way to work it is to slide your fingers underneath it like a pair of forks[1], with your thumbs on top[2], swing it upwards and then slap it back down, away from you, onto the counter (it will almost be too sticky to lift at this point). Stretch the front of the dough towards you[3], then lift it back over itself in an arc (to trap the air)[4], still stretching it forwards and sideways and tucking it in around the edges. Keep repeating this sequence[5]. At first this might seem to be too much to think about, but once you get the hang of it, you will find that you are able work the dough easily in one quick, seamless movement[6]. The dvd will help with this.

1

2

3

4

5

6

• As you work the dough it will start to come together and feel alive and elastic in your hands[7]. Keep on working it until it comes cleanly away from the counter[8], begins to look silky and feels smooth, firm-but-wobbly, and responsive[9]—you'll understand what I mean, when you feel it for yourself. I promise you the fascination with dough starts here! Once you get used to this technique, it should only take around 5 minutes, as opposed to 10–15 minutes of traditional kneading.

7

8

9

• Now you can flour the counter lightly, place the dough on top[10], and form it into a ball by folding each edge in turn into the center of the dough[11] and pressing down well with your thumb, rotating the ball as you go. Turn the whole ball over and stretch and tuck the edges under[12]. You will come across this technique in various stages throughout recipes—in each case follow this folding method.

10

11

12

Using a mixer with a dough hook

• Put the flour into your mixer bowl and rub in the yeast. Switch the mixer onto the slowest speed, add the salt and then the water, and mix for 2 minutes, then turn up to the next slowest speed and mix for another 6-7 minutes until the dough becomes smooth and elastic. Remove the dough from the bowl, transfer to a lightly floured counter and mold into a ball (page 25).

resting

• Whichever method you use, once the dough has been mixed or worked, lightly flour the inside of your mixing bowl and put the ball of dough into it. Cover with a lintfree dishtowel and rest in a draft-free place (page 20). Leave the dough for around 1 hour, until it is roughly double in volume—don't worry if this happens a bit quicker, or takes a little longer, as the dough will react slightly differently according to the temperature of your kitchen. (A few of the recipes require you to rest the dough for a shorter or longer time anyway, so check the recipe before you start.) Once the dough has rested, you are ready to continue with whatever recipe you choose.

keeping the dough going (making a ferment)

If you keep back a 7-ounce piece of dough when you make your first batch of bread, you can leave that piece in the refrigerator, "refreshing it" from time to time, to develop its flavor. Then you can add it to your next batch of dough to enhance it, keep back another 7-ounce piece of that dough, and so on... that way you add more flavor and character to your dough and bread every time you bake. When you keep back your dough, put it in a bowl in the fridge, tightly covered with plastic wrap, leave it for 2 days, and add double its weight of flour (14oz.) and of water (7oz.). Mix well until you have a firm dough, then put it back in the fridge. If you aren't going to be baking for awhile, refresh it every 7-10 days. To save your fridge from being over-run by growing dough keep back 7 ounces of it (throw away the rest) and again add double the weight of flour and of water and mix it in. Some people say you should leave the dough in ambient conditions, but if you keep it in the fridge you can control the temperature much better. You are in charge, not the dough. And as you become more confident and bake more regularly, you can increase the amount of dough you refresh so you can bake bigger batches of bread. Larger quantities of dough will mature more slowly so you can leave more time between feeding. I keep up to 4$1/2$ pounds of dough in my fridge so if I go on vacation for two weeks, I don't have to worry that it will have "died" in the meantime—or take it with me in my suitcase. Don't laugh—I know people who have done it. I imagine them checking into their hotel, "Yes there is me, my wife, my kids ...and my ferment!"

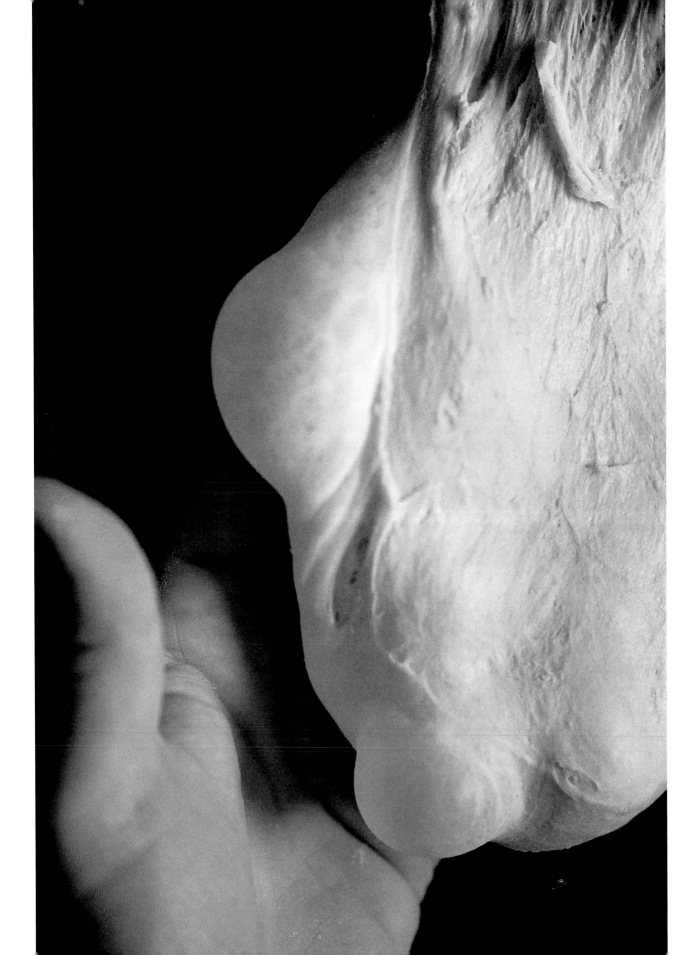

to roll into small balls

• After you have rested the dough, turn it out onto your counter. First flatten the dough with the heel of your hand into a rough oval shape. Fold one side of the flattened dough into the middle and use the heel of your hand to press it down and seal, then fold the other side into the middle and again press down firmly to seal. Finally fold in half lengthwise so you end up with a long sausage shape and seal the long edge. By folding and pressing in this way—a technique that is repeated for many of the breads that are "molded" (shaped)— you give the dough extra strength and "backbone". Turn over so it is seam-side-down.

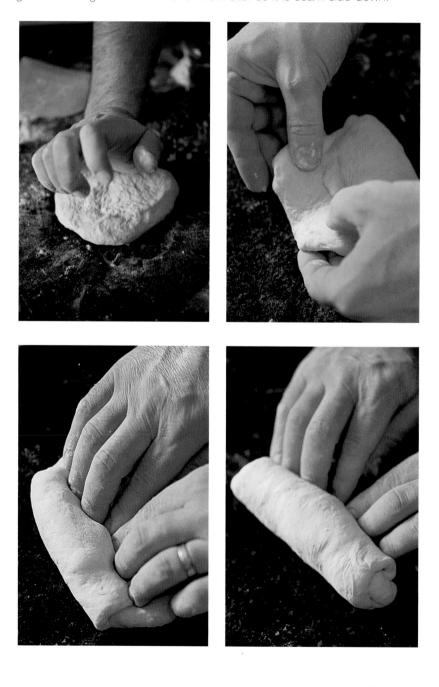

• Cut the log of dough into equal pieces as required for each recipe. To make these into small balls, you start off by using the same technique as for forming the worked dough into a ball before resting, i.e., fold each edge in turn into the center of the dough and press down well with your thumb, or fingers, rotating the ball as you go (page 25). Turn the ball over and roll it in the palm of your hand, smoothing and easing the edges underneath. If the recipe calls for a tight ball then fold in a few more times into the center.

to shape into rolls

• Form each piece into balls (page 28). Flatten each ball into a circle with your fingers, then repeat the folding technique: fold one third into the center and press down and seal with the side of your thumb, or heel of your hand, whichever feels more comfortable. Fold in the opposite third and seal again. Fold the roll in half lengthwise and seal the 2 sides together. Finally seal both ends. With the seam underneath, roll the dough evenly with your hands, easing the ends outwards, so that they become pointed.

to shape into loaves

• The technique is similar to shaping rolls, except you will be using one big ball of dough or two, according to the recipe. First flatten the ball of dough a little with the heel of your hand. Fold one edge into the center and press down with the heel of your hand. Fold the other edge over into the center and press down again. Fold over in half and then press down again firmly to seal the edges. Turn over and place (seam-side-down) on a wooden peel or baking tray or in a greased loaf pan and let rise according to the recipe.

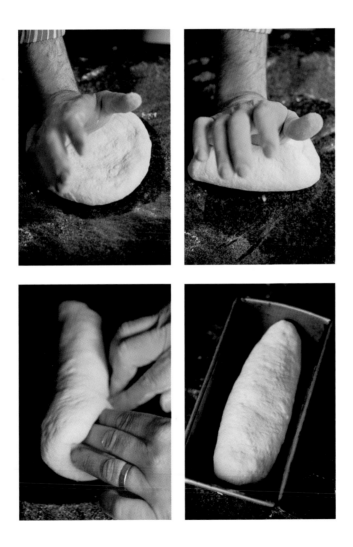

small breads are more fun...

When you make bread for the first time, I always suggest that you try some small breads first because if you make one big loaf and it collapses, you may never give it a try again. Small breads are more fun. So begin with the simplest dough of all, white dough, and I would suggest trying the fougasse—one of the easiest breads to make, and one of the biggest hits in my bread class.

1. White Dough

What is white dough? Flour, water, salt, and yeast; that's all. This is the simplest, most fundamental dough you can make. But from just four basic elements, what possibilities, what endless variations, what fun... I never stop being amazed at how much you can do with four everyday ingredients. There is something so satisfying, addictive even, about experimenting with white dough. Even my son gets excited about making this bread with his dad.

1/3 ounce (10g) Fresh yeast (preferably) or 1/4-oz. envelope active dry yeast
  (1-1 1/2 teaspoons)
18 ounces White bread flour (about 3 3/4-3 7/8 cups)
1/3 ounce (10g) Fine-grain salt (about 2 teaspoons)
12 1/2 ounces Water (or 13 fl. oz in a measuring
  cup—just over 1-1 1/2 cups, but weighing is more accurate—page 20)

Rub the yeast into the flour using your fingertips as if making a crumble. Add the salt and water. Hold the bowl with one hand and mix the ingredients around with the other (or use the rounded end of your scraper) for 2–3 minutes until the dough starts to form. Make the dough according to the method on pages 22–25. Remember to preheat the oven to 475ºF (250ºC) or as higher temperature as the oven will go. Here is a reminder of the four stages of working the dough.

1. Slide your fingers underneath with your thumbs on top.

2. Swing the dough upwards then slap it down away from you.

3. Stretch the front of the dough towards you.

4. Lift it back over itself in an arc to trap in the air.

baguette

saffron roll

pain d

breadsticks

fougas

breads

epi

lemon
roll

layered roll

gruyère &
cumin loaf

spicy
oroccan
roll

puff ball

n façon
aucaire

fougasse

When I teach people to make bread this is always one of the first recipes I get them to try because fougasses are simple, and yet so smart and impressive looking, with a texture that is crunchy on the outside and soft inside. When they come out of the oven I see everyone wearing what I call, "the fougasse grin" that says, "Look what I've made!"

In all cooking, what goes around comes around as fashions constantly change. The contemporary looking fougasses that you see—they might be leaf-shaped, or shot through with olives— are in fact just a reincarnation of an idea that has been around for a very long time. The original fougasse is a flatbread that belongs to the same family as focaccia—the word comes from the Latin word *focus* which means hearth— because the breads, which were like pancakes, were cooked under the cinders in the hearth.

I like to use maize flour for dusting this bread as it gives the crust a rich golden color and creates the impression that the fougasse has been baked in a wood-fired oven. You can make fougasses with olive, rye, or brown dough too.

Quantity: Makes 6 fougasses
Preparation: 20 minutes
Resting: 65 minutes
Baking: 10–12 minutes

1 Batch White dough (page 33) rested for 1 hour
1¹/₂ cups White flour or cornmeal for dusting

To make

• Flour the counter well. Use the rounded end of your plastic scraper to release the dough from the bowl, so that you can scoop it out easily in one piece and transfer it to the counter without stretching it. Be careful not to deflate the dough when handling it but let it spread out to cover a square of the counter. Generously flour the top of the dough, cover with a lintfree dishtowel, and let rest for another 5 minutes.

• Using the flat edge of your scraper, cut the dough into two rectangles, and then cut each piece again into three roughly rectangular pieces. Again handle the dough as gently as you can so that it stays as light and full of air as possible. Keep the pieces well floured.

• Take one of the pieces of dough and use the flat edge of your scraper to make a large diagonal cut across the center, making sure that you don't go right to the edges of the dough, but cut all the way through the dough onto your counter. Then make three smaller diagonal cuts fanning out on each side of the central one. Put your fingers into the slits and gently open them out to form holes. Be bold. In my classes, sometimes people try to make complicated patterns with lots of little cuts but, of course when the dough bakes, they will close up. It is better to make fewer cuts and really open out the holes.

• Lift onto a lightly floured wooden peel or flat-edged baking tray and from here, slide onto the hot baking stone or upturned tray in the preheated oven. Do this as quickly as possible, to avoid letting heat out of the oven. Using a water spray, mist the inside of the oven with water just before closing the door. Turn the heat down to 450°F (230°C) and bake for 10–12 minutes until golden brown.

Variations: After the dough has been worked by hand or mixed, just before you let it rest, add some halved olives (buy good-quality ones with the pit in, and take the pit out yourself), roasted peppers, roasted onions, or just press some fresh rosemary or thyme leaves into each fougasse before baking.

Part-baking for the freezer: If you want to freeze your fougasse, ³/₄-bake them for 6–7 minutes then remove them from the oven, cool, wrap in freezer bags, and freeze. To use, bake from frozen for 12 minutes at 400°F (200°C).

puff balls

These crispy thin balls of dough are a play on the classic idea of a salad with croûtons—but this way the bread is actually encasing the salad, one which can be as simple as aromatic greens and herbs, or if you want to be smart you could add some shaved truffle. The idea is to crack open the tops, like boiled eggs. The salad will spring out from the inside—I promise you, it always gets a good reaction!

Remember that whatever you use as a filling shouldn't have any dressing, or the puff ball will become soggy. You can serve the dressing separately, for everyone to add once the puff balls are cracked open. This should give enough dough to make 20 good-sized puff balls, but when you make them the first time, expect to break a few. Hopefully, you will end up with at least 10 perfect ones—you can use the broken ones as "chips" with some dipping sauces. With practice you can try shaping the dough into pillows or squares, rather than balls, or even make bite-sized ones for parties.

Quantity:	20 puff balls or 10 puff balls	**1 Batch** White dough (page 33)
	and a bowlful of "bread chips"	rested for 20 minutes
Preparation:	20 minutes	Flour for dusting
Resting:	25 minutes	Salad of your choice
Baking:	30 minutes	

To make

• Use the rounded end of your plastic scraper to scoop the dough from the bowl onto a clean counter, and use the flat edge to divide it into equal pieces (about 40g each).

• Round each piece of dough into a small ball (page 28), cover with a lintfree dishtowel and let it rest for another 5 minutes.

• Make sure there are no tiny pieces of dried dough on the counter or rolling pin, as any particles that get into the dough will stop it from puffing up. Dust your counter with some flour—sift it first, for the same reason.

• Roll out each piece of dough into a disc, turning it over a few times, and flouring well as you go. Continue rolling until the dough is really thin (about 1/16-inch—1–2mm thick).

• You will need to bake the puff balls two or three at a time, depending on the size of your oven, so slide the first two or three onto a wooden peel or flat-edged baking tray, and use this to transfer the dough onto the baking stone or upturned tray in the preheated oven. Bake for about 3–4 minutes. The puff balls should inflate very quickly and are ready when they are completely puffed up, golden, and sound hollow if you tap them (very!) gently with your finger.

• Carefully remove each one from the oven and cool on a wire rack. The puff balls are at their best about 3–4 hours after baking, but can be kept for a couple of days in an airtight tin. Don't store in a plastic bag or they will soften.

To serve

At the last minute, brush a small circle of the bottom with water to soften the crust, then carefully cut out this softened disc with a sharp knife. Just before serving, push a good quantity of salad gently into each puff ball. Let everyone break the tops with a spoon or fork, and the salad will spring out.

Note: You can roll and bake in a continual process, rolling out one ball, putting it in the oven, then rolling out the next as the first one bakes, and so on.

bread shots

These are tiny pieces of dough, which make unusual little canapés to pass around with drinks. You simply roll out the pieces into little balls—try to do it as tightly as possible—then press your finger, or the end of a wooden spoon handle, into the center to make a well, so that you can put in a filling such as cheese, pesto, or even a walnut half or olive. When you leave the balls to rise, the dough will rise up around the filling.

Quantity: About 30 bread shots
Preparation: 20 minutes
Resting: 1¼ hours
2nd Rising: 45 minutes
Baking: 8–10 minutes

1 Batch White dough (page 33) rested for 1 hour
Flour for dusting
A little Olive oil for greasing plus extra-virgin olive oil
   for finishing

A selection of 2 or more fillings:
- Pesto (page 76)
- Tomato paste (page 76) or mix some finely chopped herbs into some good-quality tomato paste
- Olive paste (page 122)
- Cheese: Choose a strong-flavored mature hard cheese, cut into ½-inch (1cm) cubes
- Walnut halves
- Good-quality, whole, pitted olives

To make
- With the help of the rounded end of your plastic scraper, turn the rested dough out onto a clean counter and, with the flat edge, divide it first into 5 x 6-ounce pieces, roll each piece into a log, cut each log in half, then cut each half into three, to make 30 pieces. Roll each piece into a tight, smooth ball (page 28). Place the balls onto a flat-edged baking tray that has been lightly greased with oil (make sure there is space between them or they will touch as they rise) and let them rest for 15 minutes. Dip the handle of a wooden spoon or your index finger into the flour and then push it into the center of the first ball. Put a little of your chosen filling into the well you have made. Repeat with the remaining balls. Let the balls rise for 45 minutes on a baking tray, covered with a lintfree dishtowel.

- Put the tray into the preheated oven and mist the inside with a water spray. Turn down the heat to 425ºF (220°C) and bake for 8–10 minutes until they are light golden brown. Remove and let cool a little, so that they are just warm before serving. Brush with a little olive oil to give a nice sheen and an extra layer of flavor.

Part-baking in advance: Bake the shots for 4 minutes, leave to cool and store in a plastic bag in the fridge. When you are ready to serve, put them back in the oven (again at 425ºF) for a few minutes until they color.

layered rolls

These are really striking but very simple to make because you don't have to do any "molding" or shaping of the dough. You just roll it out, then cut it into discs with a cutter, and bake the discs one on top of the other. Such a simple idea, which you could do alternating two different types of dough: perhaps using some plain and some flavored with Morrocan spice (page 53) or saffron (page 63).

Quantity:	10–12 rolls	**1 Batch** White dough (page 33) rested for 1 hour
Preparation:	20 minutes	Flour for dusting
Resting:	1 hour	
2nd Rising:	45 minutes	
Baking:	10–12 minutes	

To make

• Flour the counter evenly and, with the help of the rounded end of your scraper turn the dough out onto it. Flatten the dough a little with your hands and then roll it out to a thickness of about $1/4$ inch (5mm).

• Use the cutter to cut out circles (or squares) and layer four pieces (brushed with a little water) on top of each other to make each roll.

• Place them on a flat-edged cookie sheet or upside-down baking tray and let it rise for 45 minutes.

• Transfer to your baking stone/upturned tray in the preheated oven. Mist the inside of the oven with a water spray just before closing the door. Turn down the heat to 450ºF (230°C) and bake for 10–12 minutes until deep golden. Cool on a wire rack.

lemon rolls

Lemon is a flavor that works particularly well with bread and, because you use the zest, the delicate, fragrant taste really shines through. I love these rolls in summer with a big bowl of salad, or even filled with smoked salmon. Of course you can make very simple rolls, without any lemon. And you can use any of the other doughs in the other chapters to make different flavored rolls.

Quantity:	9–10 rolls	**1 Batch** White dough (page 33)
Preparation:	20 minutes	**Zest of 2** large lemons
Resting:	65 minutes	Flour for dusting
2nd Rising:	1 hour	
Baking:	9–10 minutes	

To prepare

Add the zest of the lemons to the dough just before you finish working it by hand or mixing in a mixer, and ensure that the zest is evenly distributed through the dough. Form the dough into a ball (page 25) and place it into a lightly floured bowl to rest for 1 hour.

To make

• With the help of the rounded end of your scraper, turn the rested dough out onto a lightly floured counter. Cut into 9–10 pieces and form into balls (page 28). Cover with a lintfree dishtowel and let it rest for 5 minutes. Shape the balls into rolls (page 30). Line a tray with a clean lintfree dishtowel and lightly flour it. Lay the rolls (seam-side–down), two abreast, parallel to the short edge of the dishtowel and then make a pleat in the towel fabric to form a barrier between these rolls and the next two. Pleat again and repeat until all the rolls are laid out on the tray. Cover with another towel. Let them rise for about 1 hour in a warm and draft-free place until the rolls have nearly doubled in volume.

• Place the rolls on a wooden peel or flat baking tray. Score the tops of the rolls with a razor blade or very sharp knife in a leaf pattern, i.e., one slash down the center and three small ones fanning out on either side. Slide onto the baking stone/upturned tray in the preheated oven, mist the inside with a water spray and turn down the heat to 425°F (220°C). Bake for 9–10 minutes until golden brown.

Part-baking for the freezer: Bake the rolls for 5–6 minutes at 425°F (220°C), and then cool completely before freezing. To serve, bake from frozen at 410°F (210°C) for 8–10 minutes until golden.

sesame & anise breadsticks

I made this bread because I love sesame seeds and I love anise—it's as simple as that. Perhaps it is to do with memories of drinking pastis in the sunshine, but I think these little sticks are great with an aperitif. Because the recipe only uses a half quantity of white dough I often make a full quantity and use the rest to make the variation that follows, with olives, herbs, and Romano pecorino. These breadsticks are a little chunkier than the Italian version (grissini), with slightly more of a bready texture. I like them quite soft and chewy—but the longer you bake them the crispier they will become.

Quantity:	18–20 breadsticks	
Preparation:	20 minutes	
Resting:	1 hour	
2nd Rising:	10–15 minutes	
Baking:	8–10 minutes	

1/2 Batch White dough (page 33) rested for 1 hour
5 Star anise or 5g star anise powder
  (about 1 teaspoon)
Heaped 1/3 cup Sesame seeds
Flour for dusting

To prepare
Grind the star anise using a mortar and pestle and sift the powder through a fine sieve or sifter. Mix it with the sesame seeds on a tray.

To make
• With the rounded end of your scraper, turn the dough out onto the lightly floured counter and flatten it with your hand into a rectangle about 6 x 12 inches (15cm x 30cm) and about 1/2-inch (1cm) thick. Sprinkle some of the seed mixture on top and press gently into the dough. Fold one third of the square into the center, pressing down with your fingertips, sprinkle some more of the seed mixture on top, and fold the opposite third of the dough over on top, as if folding a letter to put into an envelope. Press down again. Sprinkle some more of the seed mixture on top and press gently into the dough. With the flat edge of your scraper, cut the dough widthwise into 10–12 strips

about 1/2-inch (1cm) wide. Twist each strip, stretching it to the length of your baking tray and roll it in the remaining sesame seed mixture. Place the strips on a cookie sheet leaving a gap between each one. Let rise for 10–15 minutes. Put into the preheated oven, mist the inside with a water spray and bake them for 8–10 minutes until golden brown.

olive, herb, & romano sticks

I love the flavors of these breadsticks—very southern Mediterranean. When we make them in the bread class people are enchanted by them. They look really smart on the table at lunch, or at a barbeque. I use purple Greek Kalamata olives, but you can substitute something similar: just don't buy cheap black shiny olives, which are really green olives subjected to oxygen to turn them black, and then coated with gum to keep them glossy. Buy them whole and take out the pits yourself—that way you will keep in all the flavor. Sometimes I make this with an herbes de Provence mix that has lavender in it, which I think is beautiful—but I know lavender is an acquired taste. If you like, you can serve the breadsticks with a little dish of good extra-virgin olive oil to dip them into.

Quantity:	12 breadsticks	**1/2 Batch** White dough (page 33) rested for 1 hour
Preparation:	20 minutes	**3/4 cup** Purple olives, such as Kalamata, with pits in
Resting:	1 hour	**1 cup** grated Romano cheese (or Parmesan, if you prefer)
2nd Rising:	30–45 minutes	**1 teaspoon** Good herbes de Provence
Baking:	10–12 minutes	Cornmeal for dusting

To prepare

Pit the olives and cut each one roughly into three. Mix the olives, cheese, and herbs together in a bowl.

To make

• With the help of the rounded end of your scraper, turn the dough out onto the counter, lightly dusted with cornmeal. Using your hand, flatten out into a rectangle about 3/4-inch (2cm) thick. Sprinkle the cheese and olive mixture on top and press it into the dough with your fingertips. Fold one third of the dough into the center and press down with your fingertips. Then fold the opposite side over on top (as if you were folding a letter to put into an envelope). Press with the palms of your hands to work the olives into the dough. With the flat edge of your scraper, cut the dough widthwise into 10–12 strips about 1/2-inch (1cm) wide. Flour the counter with cornmeal. Twist each strip and roll them a little on the counter so they stretch to the length of your baking tray (nonstick, or covered with foil so that the cheese in the dough doesn't stick to the tray) and place the strips on top, leaving a good gap between each one. Cover with a lintfree dishtowel and let rise for 30–45 minutes. Put into the preheated oven. Mist the inside with a water spray, then bake them for 10–12 minutes until golden brown. Use a spatula to lift them from the baking tray. Cool on a wire rack.

spicy moroccan rolls

One day I bought a package of the traditional Moroccan spice mix, Ras-el-Hanout, and tried adding some of it to my bread dough. The flavors—which include the likes of cinnamon, nutmeg, turmeric, cardamom seeds, black pepper, and cloves—came through really well. When I think of Morocco, I think of those wonderful squashy cushions that people sit on—so I decided to make these rolls in a similar shape. If you are making a tagine, or any dish using Moroccan spices, these would make a great accompaniment.

Quantity:	20 small rolls	**1 Batch** White dough (page 33)	
Preparation:	20 minutes	**1 ounce** Moroccan spice blend (Ras-el-Hanout)—	
Resting:	45 minutes	about $1/4$ cup	
2nd Rising:	30–45 minutes	**3$1/2$ ounces** Sesame seeds (about $3/4$ cup)	
Baking:	10–12 minutes	Flour for dusting	

To prepare

• Just before you have finished working the dough by hand, or at the end of mixing time in the mixer, add the spices and work or mix the dough a little more to make sure they are evenly distributed. Shape into a ball (page 25), cover with a lintfree dishtowel and let rest for 45 minutes.

To make

• Turn the dough out onto a lightly floured counter and flatten a little with the palm of your hand.

• Divide the dough into two and mold each piece into a log shape (using the folding technique on page 28). Divide each log into 10 equal rolls—they will look a bit like overgrown marshmallows. Brush one cut side of each roll with water and then dip them into a bowl containing the sesame seeds.

• Cover with a lintfree dishtowel and leat rise for 30–45 minutes or until the rolls have nearly doubled in size.

• Mist the inside of your preheated oven with a water spray, and slide the rolls onto your baking stone/upturned baking tray. Bake them for 10–12 minutes. Remove from the oven and cool on a wire rack.

baguettes

In France the word baguette has a very strict meaning: a baguette must weigh 320g (about 11½ oz.) and there must be seven cuts along the top, as opposed to five on le pain. The point of the cuts is to let the crust burst open so that it is good and crunchy. Every baker cuts the dough in his own way—it is his signature, which everyone else in the bakery recognizes. But you don't need to worry about rules. Just try making some small baguettes first, and when you mold the bread, do it as tightly as you can; then, just before you put the bread into the oven, spray the oven with water to create steam—these details will help you to create the fantastic thick crust that a good baguette should have. In France, everyone likes their baguette baked differently. Personally I like the crust to be deep golden, not pale and insipid as you often see in this country (other people prefer them well cooked—*bien cuit*). Resting the bread for a minimum of 1 hour will give you the right light, airy texture inside, with plenty of holes running through the bread.

   Every time you make a baguette, keep back a piece (page 26) and add it to your next batch of dough; that way you will infuse more and more flavor into it each time you bake.

Quantity:	4 large or 8 mini baguettes
Preparation:	20 minutes
Resting:	65 minutes
2nd Rising:	45–60 minutes
Baking:	12 minutes

1 Batch White dough (page 33) rested for 1 hour
Flour for dusting

To prepare
Line a baking tray with a lightly floured lintfree dishtowel.

To make
• With the help of the rounded end of your scraper, turn the dough out onto a floured counter. Using the sharp side of your scraper cut it into 4 pieces (weighing about 8 ounces each) if you are making full-sized baguettes or 8 (weighing about 4 ounces each) for the mini baguettes. Roll each piece into a ball (page 28) and let them rest for another 5 minutes.

• Lightly dust the counter with flour. To mold the baguettes, take the first ball, turn it rounded side down and then flatten it with the heel of your hand into a rough oval shape. Fold one side of your flattened dough into the middle and again use the heel of your hand, or thumb, to press it down and seal. Bring the other side over to the middle and again press down to seal. By folding and pressing in this way, you give the dough some extra strength down the spine of the baguette. Finally, fold in half lengthwise and seal the edges so you end up with a long log shape. Roll each baguette a little to shape and extend it to the length of your towel-lined baking tray. Repeat with the other balls of dough.

• Lay the baguettes on the towel on your baking tray, making a pleat in the towel between each one (to stop them touching as they rise). Cover with another towel and let rise for 45–60 minutes, or until they have nearly doubled in volume.

• Transfer the baguettes to a very lightly floured wooden peel or flat-edged cookie sheet. Using a razor blade or sharp knife, make 5 or 6 diagonal cuts across the top of the baguettes. Make the cuts swiftly and cleanly, taking care not to drag the dough.

• The crust on your baguettes will be be crunchier if you bake them with a little steam, so mist the inside of the preheated oven using a water spray just before putting them in. Slide them onto your baking stone or tray in the oven. Spray again with water just before closing the door and bake for 10–12 minutes until the crust is a nice deep golden color. (Once you have closed the door, do not open it for the first 4–5 minutes so that you maintain the heat needed to form the crust.)

Variation: Epis

You see these all the time in French bakeries. Because there is more exposed surface area, they are even more crusty than the traditional baguette, and great to put in the middle of the table, letting people break off the "ears."

Follow the method for baguettes up to the point of laying the bread on a lightly floured flat baking tray. With a pair of scissors, held at a 45° angle to the dough, start at one end of the baguette and make snips (cutting three quarters of the way through the dough) at intervals all the way down the center. This will create "V" shaped points of dough which you can push to alternate sides of the bread, so that it looks like a wheatsheaf. Bake, with steam (as above), for 10–12 minutes.

gruyère cheese & cumin bread

Cumin is a favorite spice of mine—I think its warmth marries brilliantly with gruyère. I love to slice this bread and then use it instead of the more traditional Pain de Mie (page 64) to make croque monsieurs.

Quantity:	3 loaves	**1 Batch** White dough (page 33) rested for 1 hour
Preparation:	20 minutes	**Scant ¹/₂ teaspoon** Cumin seeds
Resting:	1¹/₂ hours	**Scant ¹/₂ teaspoon** Cumin powder
2nd Rising:	1–1¹/₂ hours	**9 ounces (250g)** Gruyère cheese, coarsely grated
Baking:	15–20 minutes	(about 2 cups)
		Flour for dusting
		A little butter for greasing

To prepare

Take 3 x 1-pound loaf pans (8-8¹/₂ inches long) and grease the insides with butter, then line with parchment paper.

To make

• With the help of the rounded end of your scraper, turn the dough out onto a lightly floured counter and flatten with the base of your hands to about ¹/₂-inch (1cm) thick. Mix the cumin seeds and powder together and sprinkle on top of the dough. Sprinkle the cheese on top and work this, and the cumin, into the dough by pressing firmly with your fingers. Fold a third of the dough into the center, and then fold the other third over the top, to ensure that the cheese is evenly distributed through the dough. Then form the dough into a ball (page 25) and let it rest for another 30 minutes.

• Divide the dough into three, mold each piece lightly into a loaf shape (page 31), and put one into each prepared pan. With a razor blade or sharp knife, cut the top of each loaf diagonally four or five times. Cover with a lintfree dishtowel and let rise for 1–1¹/₂ hours until the loaves have nearly doubled in volume. The exact time taken will depend on the temperature of your rising place.

• Put the pans into the preheated oven, mist the inside with a water spray and turn down the heat to 410°F (210°C). Bake for 15–20 minutes until golden brown on top. Remove the loaves from the pans—check that the bottom is golden brown, if not, return to the oven without the pan for a few minutes. Cool on a wire rack.

pain façon beaucaire

The true Pain Beaucaire originates on the Côte d'Azur, and uses a special local wheat. This version uses white dough, but with the same folding technique, which looks really smart. I've found that once people get the hang of how easy it is to do, without having to mold the dough, they make it time and time again. Later on, when you feel confident to make pain de campagne (page 132), you can use the same folding technique with that dough.

Quantity:	8 small rolls	**1 Batch** White dough (page 33) rested for 1 hour
Preparation:	20 minutes	Cornmeal or whole-wheat flour for dusting
Resting:	1 hour	White flour for dusting
2nd Rising:	30 minutes	
Baking:	10–12 minutes	

To make

• With the help of the rounded end of your scraper, turn out the dough and flatten out with your hands into a rectangle. Brush with a little water and sprinkle some or whole-wheat flour or cornmeal on top. Fold over the dough lengthwise, stopping about 1 inch (2.5–3cm) before the edge. Brush this edge with water, fold it back over the dough, and seal.

• Lay a lintfree dishtowel on the counter and sprinkle liberally with white flour. Place the dough, seam-side-down, on the towel and flour the exposed surface. Cover with another lintfree dishtowel and let it rise for 30 minutes somewhere warm and draft-free or until it has nearly doubled in size.

• With a sharp serrated knife, cut the dough widthwise into 1-inch (3cm) slices. Place the pieces on a baking tray on their side, open out gently (so they look a bit like ring doughnuts but with a smaller and thinner hole), and bake in the preheated oven for 10–12 minutes or until golden brown.

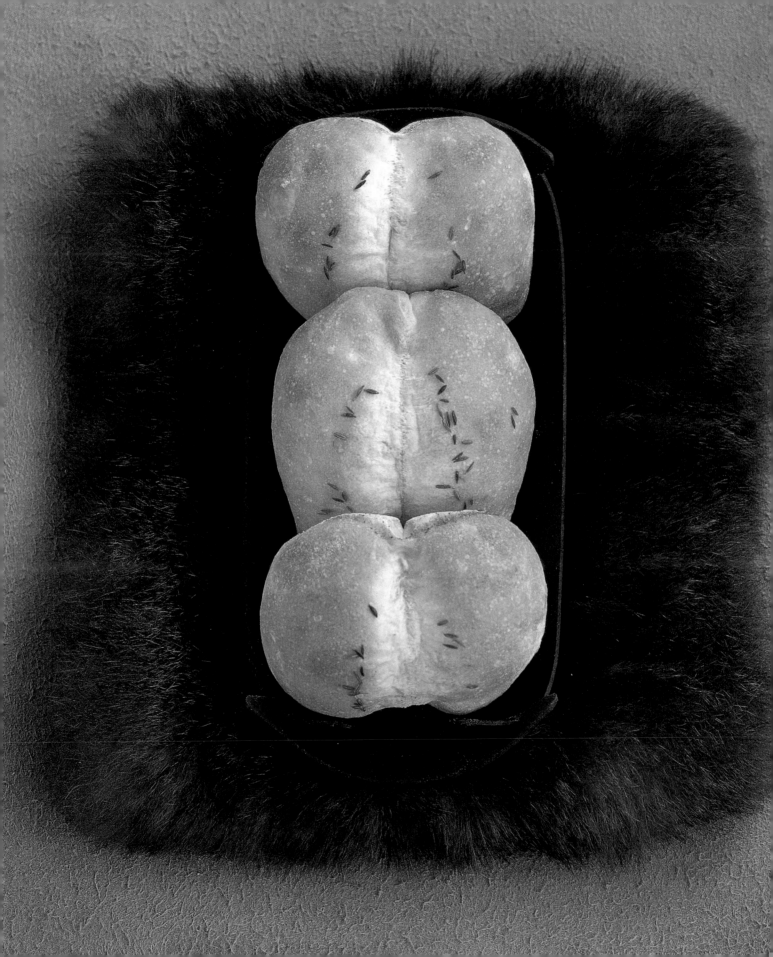

saffron rolls

Saffron (the dried stigma of a particular type of crocus) is another of those luxurious, glamorous ingredients that if you use with too heavy a hand can taste overpowering (and look too yellow) but, used in bread as a background flavor, it gives a lovely warm and delicate note. I love this bread with seafood chowder, or a fish stew like bouillabaisse—or you can use it to make crab or shrimp salad sandwiches. Try to use saffron strands, rather than powder, as they give a smarter appearance to the bread, and a richer flavor.

Quantity:	9 or 10 rolls	**1 Batch** White dough (page 33)
Preparation:	20 minutes	**Pinch** of Saffron strands (If you can't get strands,
Resting:	1 hour	powdered saffron will do)
2nd Rising:	45 minutes	**A few** Cumin seeds
Baking:	12 minutes	Flour for dusting

To prepare

When making the dough, dilute a few strands of saffron, or powder, in the water before mixing the dough, then continue as usual, letting the dough rest for 1 hour. Line a baking tray with a lintfree dishtowel and dust with flour.

To make

• With the help of the rounded end of your scraper, turn out the dough, and with your hand, flatten into a rectangle. Fold one third of the dough into the center and press down with your fingertips; fold the opposite side over on top (as if you were folding a letter to put into an envelope). With the flat edge of your scraper, cut into 9 or 10 pieces (weighing about 3–4 ounces each), and mold each one into a ball (page 28). Flour the top of each ball and then place a floured rolling pin across the center and press down firmly. The dough will rise up either side of the indent you have made, leaving you with a roll that resembles a coffee bean.

• Lay the rolls, two abreast, on the lined baking tray, making a pleat in the towel between each pair of rolls, cover with another towel, and let them rise for 45 minutes.

• Sprinkle a few cumin seeds on top of each roll, then slide onto your baking stone/upturned tray in the preheated oven. Mist the inside with a water spray and turn down the heat to 425°F (220°C). Bake for 12 minutes. Cool on a wire rack.

pain de mie/ everyday loaves

This is as close as you get to a sliced loaf in France; however, the dough is enriched with milk, butter, and sugar. This is one of the few breads in France that is baked in a pan. "Mie" means crumb, because this bread is all about the crumb rather than the crust ("croûte"). It is traditionally used for canapés and small toasts, where you don't want a crusty edge. So if you have a pan with a lid, bake it in that, or put a tray on top for most of the baking time, to prevent a proper crust from forming. This is also the typical bread to use for a croque monsieur (you could also use the Gruyère cheese and Cumin bread, page 58, or Pain Viennois—made in a pan, page 154), the snack that all French kids grow up with: 2 slices spread with a little béchamel (page 150), filled with a layer of ham, topped with a thick layer of béchamel and some grated Gruyère cheese, and put into a preheated oven at 400ºF (200ºC) for about 12 minutes until the cheese melts and turns golden —brilliant! I also use Pain de Mie to make summer pudding—my favorite British dessert (bread and butter pudding in winter; summer pudding in summer—the best!); I love it so much that Jo and I even served it at our wedding.

Quantity:	2 loaves
Preparation:	20 minutes
Resting:	1 hour
2nd Rising:	1 hour
Baking:	25–30 minutes

2 teaspoons Unsalted butter

$2/3$ ounce (20g) Fresh yeast (preferably) or $1/4$-ounce (7g) envelope active dry yeast ($1^1/2$ teaspoons)

18 ounces White bread flour (about $3^3/4$-$3^7/8$ cups)

2 ounces Whole milk (about 4 tablespoons)

$10^1/2$ ounces Water (just under 12fl. oz. in a glass measuring cup

A little butter for greasing

To prepare

Grease 2 x 1-pound loaf pans with a little butter.

Make the dough according to the method on page 33, adding the butter with the yeast (rubbing them both in together) and the milk with the water, and let the dough rest for 1 hour.

To make

• With the help of the rounded edge of your scraper, turn out the dough onto a floured surface, and divide the dough into two equal pieces. Mold each piece very tightly into a loaf shape (page 31).

• Once the loaves are in their pans, let them rise in a warm draft-free place for 1 hour. Keep a close eye on the loaves while they are rising and when the dough is level with the top of the pan, cover with a lid or heavy tray weighed down so the dough can't rise any further.

• Put the pans into the preheated oven. Tturn down the heat to 425ºF (220°C). Bake the loaves for 20–25 minutes, covered, and then another 4–5 minutes uncovered. Remove the loaves from the pans and let cool.

summer pudding (serves 4-6)

Cut 6-8 slices of stale pain de mie—about 1/2-inch (11/2 cm) thick—and trim off the crusts. Keep back a couple of slices (for the lid) and use the rest to line the bottom and sides of a pudding mold or ovenproof bowl—make sure the inside of the bowl is completely covered (trim the bread to shape if necessary so that it fits closely together).

Remove the stalks and/or pits from 11/4 pounds (600g) mixed soft fruits (include as many different fruits as you are able to get hold of from strawberries, raspberries, blackberries, red currants, black currants, and sweet black cherries but avoid adding too many black currants as they can overpower the other fruits).

Put the fruit in a wide, heavy pan, add 1/2 cup caster sugar, bring to a boil over low heat and cook for a couple of minutes until the sugar has dissolved and the fruit has just started to soften and release its juice. Remove from the heat. Set aside 3 or 4 tablespoons of the juice, then spoon the fruit and the rest of the juice into the prepared bowl and cover with the remaining slices of bread. Place a plate, the same size as the rim of the bowl, on top of the pudding and weigh it down (a can or jar will do). Place the bowl, with the weight on top, in the fridge and let it chill for at least 6 hours but preferably overnight.

To serve, remove the weight and the plate and slide a pastry spatula around the inside of the bowl to release the pudding. Cover the bowl with a serving plate and invert the bowl to turn the pudding out onto the plate. Add 2 tablespoons crème de cassis to the reserved juices then carefully pour them over the pudding so that all of the bread is soaked through and colored.

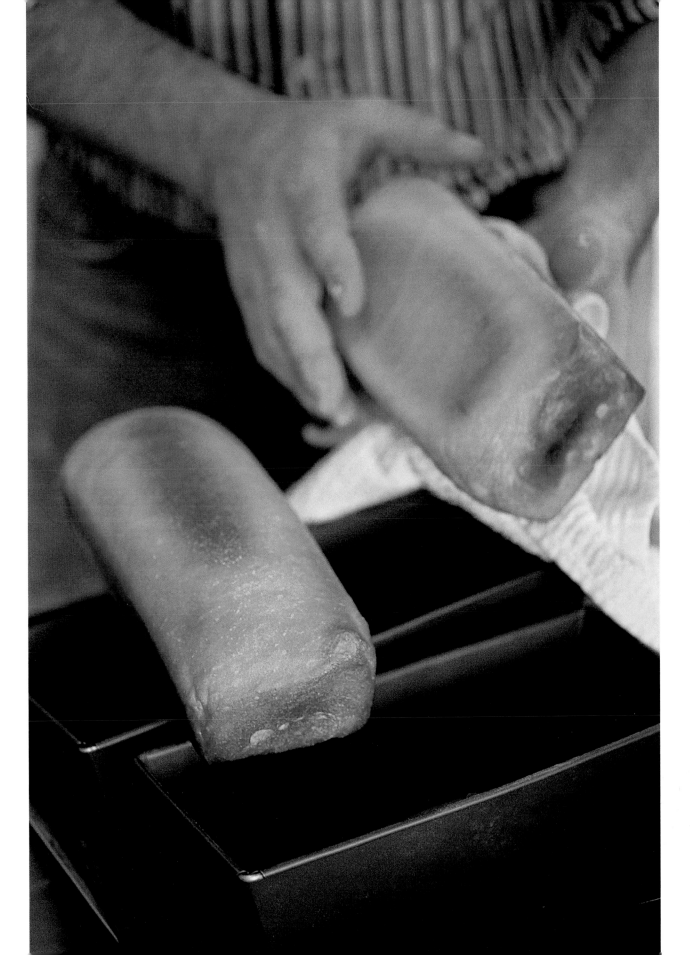

2. Olive Dough

olive oil: emollient; prized

This takes the basic White Dough on a stage further, adding olive oil which gives a lovely softness to the dough, making it very resilient, and resulting in bread with a fantastic texture and flavor, which also freezes well. There is also a recipe for ciabatta that uses avocado oil, to make a wonderfully tasty variation.

I like to use a light fruity olive oil, not a peppery intense one—and I also like to use a little semolina in the dough, to add character to the bread. The dough will feel slightly wetter than the white dough we made in the previous chapter, but once you have mastered the technique of working it, it will come together beautifully.

18 ounces Bread flour (about $3^3/_4$–$3^7/_8$ cups)
2 tablespoons Coarse semolina
$^1/_2$ ounce (15g) Fresh yeast preferably or $^1/_4$-oz. (7g) envelope active dry yeast ($1^1/_2$ teaspoons)
$^1/_3$ ounce Salt (about 2 teaspoons fine-grain)
2 ounces Good-quality extra-virgin olive oil (about 5 tablespoons)
$11^1/_2$ ounces Water (just over 12fl. oz. in a glass measuring cup)

Preheat the oven to 475°F (250°C). Mix the bread flour and semolina together and rub in the yeast, using your fingertips as if making a crumble. Add the salt, olive oil, and water, then continue, according to the method on pages 22–25.

flatbread

soup bc

prosciutto,
parmesan,
& pine nut
slices

pizza

pancetta & mixed olive bread

tomato, garlic, & basil bread

ciabatta

coarse salt & rosemary focaccia

coarse salt & rosemary focaccia

This is such an easy, popular bread to make and makes a generous slab that everyone can share. Just as every French baker has his own way of making a baguette, I'm sure every Italian baker lends his own individual style to focaccia. I'm not pretending that this is an authentic Italian recipe—just my way of making a fantastic Italian style of bread.

Quantity:	1 large slab	
Preparation:	20 minutes	
Resting:	2¼ hours	
2nd Rising:	45 minutes	
Baking:	25–30 minutes	

1 Batch Olive dough (page 69) rested for 1 hour
4 tablespoons Olive oil plus a little extra
A few sprigs of Fresh rosemary
Good-quality coarse salt, e.g. kosher salt

To make

• With the help of the rounded end of your scraper, turn the dough out onto an oiled tray. Drizzle the oil over the dough, then, using your fingers, push and prod the dough so that it spreads from the center towards the edges of the tray—but try not to stretch or pull it. Cover with a lintfree dishtowel and let it rest somewhere warm and draft-free for 45 minutes.

• Prod the dough again, dimpling it with your fingertips, and rest for 30 minutes more.

• Take the leaves off the sprigs of rosemary and push them evenly into the dough. Sprinkle the coarse salt over it and immediately put into the preheated oven. Turn down the heat to 425°F (220°C) and bake it for 25–30 minutes, until it is light golden brown. Remove from the oven and slide onto a wire rack to cool. Brush with a little more olive oil while it's still hot.

Variation: Pesto, Olive, & Pepperdew
Pepperdew are little sweet yet piquant, and quite mild peppers, that come in a jar—you should be able to find them in most supermarkets. If you prefer something hotter, use red chilies instead. Follow the recipe above, but instead of topping with rosemary and coarse salt, cut 20 cherry tomatoes in half, drain a jar of pepperdew, and tear the peppers into pieces with your fingers. Remove the pits from a handful of Kalamata olives. Spread 4 tablespoons fresh pesto (page 76) onto the rested dough and work it evenly into the dough with your fingertips. Sprinkle the peppers on top, then the tomatoes, and finally the olives. Push all of these ingredients gently into the dough. Leave to prove for 45 minutes and bake and finish with oil as above.

tomato, garlic, & basil bread

Three beautiful flavors that work even better together and make a lovely moist bread that looks brilliantly colo`rful, is a lot more interesting than garlic bread, and more tasty than tomato bread (much of which is made commercially with pre-mixed flavoring that reminds me of cheap tomato soup). When you dust the bread in cornmeal it gives the finished loaf a rich color.

Quantity:	3 loaves	**1 Batch** Olive dough (page 69) rested for 1 hour
Preparation:	20 minutes	**4 ounces** Oven-dried tomatoes (page 76)
Resting:	1 hour	**20 cloves** Roasted garlic (page 76)
2nd Rising:	30 minutes	**Large bunch** of fresh basil—leaves only
Baking:	20–25 minutes	A little extra-virgin olive oil to finish
		Flour for dusting (either white or cornmeal)

To make

• Flour your work surface generously with white flour or cornmeal. With the help of the rounded end of your scraper, turn the rested dough out onto the work surface so that the sticky underside is uppermost. Sprinkle a little flour onto the dough and then, using your fingertips, spread it out gently into a rectangle about 14 x 10 inches (35 x 25cm), prodding it gently, so you dimple it with your fingertips.

• Brush the excess flour from the top of the dough. Spread the tomatoes evenly over it and push them gently into it using your fingertips. Do the same with the garlic and then the basil leaves.

• Fold the right-hand third of the rectangle into the center. Repeat with the left-hand third so that you end up with a smaller rectangle. Press the dough gently with your fingertips to work the additional ingredients better into the dough and tuck under the edges neatly all the way around.

• Cut the dough crosswise into three equal pieces. Tuck the dough under one of the cut sides of the middle piece. Lightly oil a baking tray. Place the three pieces on it, cut-side up (so that you can see the tomato, garlic, and basil). Cover with a lintfree dishtowel and let them rise somewhere warm and draft-free for 30 minutes.

• Put into the preheated oven, turn the heat down to 425°F (220°C) and bake for 20–25 minutes until golden brown. Remove and transfer to a wire rack to cool. Brush with a little extra-virgin olive oil while still warm.

Part-baking for the freezer: If you want to freeze these loaves, bake them for 15 minutes and then let cool for at least 1 hour. Wrap them well in freezer bags. To use, put them in a preheated oven at 350°F (180°C) and bake for 12–15 minutes from frozen, or for 8–10 minutes if defrosted.

oven-dried tomatoes

Preheat the oven to 210°F (100°C). You need 1 carton/$1/2$ pound cherry tomatoes or 6–8 larger tomatoes. If you are using cherry tomatoes, cut them in half; if they are larger, quarter them and lay them on a baking tray, skin-side-down. Season with sea salt and freshly ground black pepper, and sprinkle on top a teaspoon of sugar and a couple of pinches of good-quality dried herbes de Provence (or a little fresh thyme and rosemary). Put in the preheated oven for 2 hours until dried but soft. After drying, the tomatoes should weigh about 4 ounces and will be sufficient for the recipe for Tomato, Garlic, & Basil Bread (pages 74–75). Note: The tomatoes can be packed into a clean, sterile jar and covered with olive oil. You can store them like this for several weeks. You can also blitz them in a food processor to make a really tasty tomato sauce for the pizza on page 84, or a tomato paste for the bread shots on page 44.

roasted garlic

Preheat the oven to 350°F (180°C). Put an ovenproof pan on the stove and add 5 tablespoons olive oil, 2 tablespoons butter, and a teaspoon of sugar. When the butter has melted, add 20 peeled garlic cloves and toss them in the mixture, then transfer to the oven and cook for 20–25 minutes until the garlic has caramelised and is soft enough to offer no resistance to the point of a sharp knife. Remove the pan from the oven and let the garlic cool in its cooking juices. Once cool, lift the garlic from the juices and drain on a few sheets of paper towel.

fresh pesto

An Italian would probably throw up his hands in horror, but I like to add a little squeeze of lemon into my pesto. Put 1 cup pine nuts into a food processor with 3 garlic cloves and $1^{1}/_{2}$ cups grated Parmesan and blitz for a few seconds. Add 3–4 bunches of basil (enough to fill the bowl of the food processor loosely) and blitz again until it has all been chopped. Add the juice of half a lemon and 4 tablespoons extra-virgin olive oil and blitz once more. Taste and season if necessary with sea salt and freshly ground black pepper. If the pesto is too thick add a little extra olive oil.
Note: The pesto can be kept in the fridge for a few days or in the freezer for several weeks.

soup bowl

I first thought of this after ordering an Indian take-out meal. The food was tasty, but it looked so boring in its little plastic trays. I thought how much more fun it would be to serve it in bowls made from bread, which you could flavor with a little chili or spice and then eat, as the sauces softened the bread. From the idea of a curry bowl, it was only a short step to thinking about also using the bread containers as soup bowls—a nice play on soup with bread or croûtons.

Quantity:	8 bowls	**1 Batch** Olive dough (page 69) rested for
Preparation:	30 minutes	30 minutes
Resting:	40 minutes	A little olive oil for greasing
Baking:	20–25 minutes	White flour for dusting

To prepare

Turn 8 ovenproof bowls (about 5-inch/12cm diameter) upside-dwon and lightly oil the outside. (I use a set of soup or breakfast bowls.)

To make

• With the help of the rounded end of your scraper, turn the dough out onto a lightly floured counter and divide it into 4-ounce pieces. Again lightly flour the counter. Taking one piece at a time, roll out the dough into circles. Shake off any excess flour and shape the dough circles over the upturned bowls. Press gently to ensure there are no air bubbles between the dough and the bowl. Rest for 10 minutes.

• Put (bowls upturned) into the preheated oven and turn down the heat to 400°F (200°C) and bake for 20–25 minutes until golden brown. (You will probably need to bake in 2 batches.) Remove them from the oven and let cool for a few minutes. Using a fine-bladed knife, gently loosen the bread from the bowls and ease it off. Cool on a wire rack.

For the freezer: The bowls freeze well for a few weeks. Stack them with a sheet of waxed paper between each one. Defrost for about 1 hour before warming them in the oven for 3 minutes at 350°F (180°C).

prosciutto, parmesan & pine nut slices

These are a little like savory pain aux raisins. You can even slice them in half if you like and fill them with arugula and slivers of Parmesan. I also like to make really small ones to serve with aperitifs – if you want to do this, cut the dough in half before you start, and when you roll it up, do so quite tightly to keep them small and neat (the larger ones can be a little looser).

Quantity:	12 slices
Preparation:	20 minutes
Resting:	1 hour
2nd Rising:	45 minutes
Baking:	12–15 minutes

1 Batch Olive dough (page 69) rested for 1 hour
3 1/2 ounces Parmesan cheese (about 1 1/2–1 3/4 cups)
1 cup Pine nuts
2 tablespoons Extra-virgin olive oil, plus a little extra for finishing
12 Slices of Prosciutto
Cornmeal for dusting

To prepare

Grate the Parmesan.

Scatter the pine nuts on a baking tray and toast under the broiler or in a hot oven, turning from time to time until they are toasted. Let cool.

To make

• Sprinkle the counter with cornmeal. With the help of the rounded end of your plastic scraper, turn the dough out onto the counter and with your fingers, spread it out into a rough rectangle, dimpling it as you go, and brush with olive oil.

• Mix the nuts and grated cheese together and sprinkle half evenly over the dough. Lay the prosciutto on top. Brush a little more oil over the prosciutto then spread the remaining cheese and nuts on top.

• Roll the dough up like a roulade and seal the seam by pushing down on it with your fingers. Using a sharp serrated knife, cut the dough into 3/4-inch (2cm) slices and place them on their sides on a lightly greased baking tray.

• Cover with a lintfree dishtowel and let rise for 45 minutes or until the slices have nearly doubled in volume.

• Put them in the preheated oven, turn down the heat to 460ºF (240°C) and bake for 12–15 minutes until golden brown. Remove and cool on a wire rack. Brush with a little more oil while still warm.

flatbread

This is very thin bread that you can use as a wrap or a pizza base. You can even bake it for a slightly longer time until it has completely dried, then break it up and serve with dips as a low-fat alternative to chips. You can also flavor the dough if you like—perhaps with some Thai spices or, alternatively, add a topping of fines herbes, coarse salt, black pepper, and (fresh or dried) chilies before baking.

Quantity:	4 flatbreads
Preparation:	20 minutes
Resting:	55–60 minutes
Baking:	8–10 minutes

1 Batch Olive dough (page 69) rested for
 30 minutes
Cornmeal for dusting
A little olive oil

To prepare

Lightly brush 4 nonstick 8 x 12-inch (20 x 30cm) trays with oil.

To make

• With the help of the rounded end of your scraper, turn out the dough and divide it into four equal pieces. Place a piece of dough onto a tray and, using your fingertips, push it out until it fills the tray. If the dough is very sticky, use a little cornmeal to help you to do this. Don't worry if it doesn't quite fill the tray; there is no need to force it—it will expand during resting and you will be able to spread it out to fill the tray then. Repeat with the other three pieces of dough.

• Cover with a lintfree dishtowel and rest for 15–20 minutes. Prod again with your fingertips to spread the dough out to fill the tray. Rest for a final 10 minutes before baking.

• To use as a wrap, put in the preheated oven, turn the heat down to 425°F (220°C) and bake for 8–10 minutes until very lightly colored (the color of part-baked dough). Don't bake any longer, as the bread needs to be soft enough to roll. Serve topped with fresh vine tomatoes, salad, prosciutto—the choices are endless.

To break up the bread into pieces to serve with a dip, bake for 15–18 minutes until crisp.

pizza

I don't use any semolina in this dough as I want it to be very smooth and elastic. The topping I have suggested is for a traditional margherita, but of course you can use any topping you like.

Quantity:	3 pizzas
Preparation:	15 minutes
Resting:	70 minutes
	or overnight in the fridge
Baking:	10–12 minutes

Pizza base:
1/2 ounce Fresh yeast
18 ounces Italian white bread flour (3³/₄–3⁷/₈ cups)
1/3 ounce Salt (about 2 teaspoons fine-grain)
2 ounces Olive oil
11¹/₂ ounces Water (just over 12fl. oz. in a glass measuring cup)
White flour for dusting

Topping for each pizza:
3/4 tablespoon Blitzed oven-dried tomatoes (page 76)
4 ounces Buffalo mozzarella
Bunch of Fresh basil, leaves picked

To prepare

Rub the yeast into the flour, using your fingertips as if making a crumble. Add the salt, olive oil, and water, then continue according to the method on pages 22–25. Let the dough to rest for 1 hour or, to achieve a better crust and taste, rest it overnight in the fridge. By doing this, you will enable the dough to rise very slowly and it will develop a little acidity that will improve its flavor and give a texture that is crispy on the outside and slightly chewy inside. Preheat the oven to 475°F (250°C).

To make

• With the help of the rounded end of your scraper, turn out the dough and shape into a ball (page 25) and let it rest for 10 minutes more. Lightly flour the counter and place the ball of dough onto the flour. You need to make sure that the flour is evenly distributed so that your pizza will not stick. Divide into three.

• Place the heel of your hand in the center of each piece of dough and push it away from you so that it stretches the dough out. Turn the dough slightly and repeat. Keep stretching the dough until you have a roughly circular pizza shape of about 8–9 inches (20–22cm) in diameter. The edge should be slightly thicker than the dough in the middle.

• Lift the pizza base onto a floured baking tray and spread the tomato sauce evenly over it. Sprinkle with chunks of mozzarella and shredded basil leaves. Slide the pizza onto the preheated baking tray or stone in the oven, turn the heat down to 460°F (240°C), and bake for 10–12 minutes until the edges become golden brown and crispy.

pancetta & mixed olive bread

The combination of these really earthy flavors is beautiful and just melts into the bread—
which makes fantastic sandwiches.

Quantity:	3 loaves
Preparation:	1 hour
Resting:	1½ hours
2nd Rising:	1 hour
Baking:	30–35 minutes

1 Batch Olive dough (page 69)

7 ounces Mixed (green and purple) olives, pits in

Bunch of Sage, stalks removed

1 tablespoon Oil for frying

7 ounces Diced pancetta or bacon

To prepare

Pit the olives and roughly chop the sage. Heat the olive oil in a frying pan. When it's hot, add the pancetta and stir. When the pancetta is starting to crisp, add the olives, stir, and cook over medium heat for about 2 minutes. Remove from the heat and add the sage. Stir well and spoon the mixture, including the cooking juices, into a bowl to cool.

During the last stage of working the dough by hand or mixing in a mixer, add the pancetta mixture, along with its cooking juices, and continue working/mixing the dough until the mixture is spread evenly through the dough. Lightly dust the inside of a clean bowl with flour and place the dough in it. Cover with a lintfree dishtowel and let it rest for 1 hour in a draft-free place.

To make

• Turn the dough out onto a lightly floured counter and form into a ball (page 25). Return to the bowl, cover, and let it rest for 30 minutes more.

• Flour the counter again and turn the dough out onto it. Divide it into three equal pieces of about 1 pound each. Fold one side into the middle and again use the heel of your hand, or thumb, to press it down and seal. Bring the other side over to the middle and again press down to seal. Finally fold in half lengthwise and seal the edges so you end up with a long log shape with rounded ends.

• Place the loaves on a baking tray and flour the tops with white flour or cornmeal. With a razor blade or sharp knife, make 6 or 7 diagonal cuts about ½ inch (1cm) deep across the top of each loaf. Cover the loaves with a lintfree dishtowel and let rise for about 1 hour or until they have nearly doubled in volume.

• Open the preheated oven and mist with a water spray. Place the loaves in the oven, turn down the heat to 450°F (230°C) and bake for 30–35 minutes until they are a golden brown color. Remove from the oven and cool on a wire rack.

ciabatta

The famous Italian "slipper" bread needs a ferment or "biga", as it is known in Italy, which helps to create a wonderful open structure and lightness. This is made simply with flour, water, and yeast, which you need to make up and leave for 24 hours before using. I always prefer to work any dough by hand, rather than mix it in a mixer with a dough hook, but this is a bread that really benefits from working by hand, to get as much air into it as possible. It starts off very soft and sticky, but as you work it it will become more and more elastic and come away from your fingers.

I make this with avocado oil, rather than olive oil. It is a bit more expensive, but worth trying as it makes beautiful bread and gives the dough a lovely, delicate avocado-green tinge.

		For the ferment:	**Dough:**
Quantity:	4 loaves	**12¹/₂ ounces** Flour	**1 pound** Italian bread flour
Preparation:	15 minutes	**6¹/₂ ounces** Water (about	**1/₃ ounce** Fresh yeast
Resting:	17–24 hours for the ferment	7fl. oz. in glass	**12 ounces** Water (about
	1¹/₂ hours for the dough	measuring cup)	13fl. oz. in glass
Proving:	30–45 minutes	**1/₂ teaspoon** Fresh yeast	measuring cup)
Baking:	18–20 minutes		**2 ounces** Olive oil or
			avocado oil
			1/₂ ounce Salt (about 1
			tablespoon fine-grain)
			A little olive oil or avocado oil
			for oiling
			Flour for dusting

To prepare (24 hours in advance)

Mix the ingredients for the ferment together in a mixer or by hand for about 5 minutes until you have a rough dough. Place in a bowl, cover loosely with plastic wrap and then a dishtowel and let it rest in a draft-free place for 17–24 hours.

To make

• Remember to preheat your oven to 475°F (250°C) at least 1 hour before you start making the dough to warm up the kitchen as well as the oven.

• Preferably make the dough by hand. Put the flour in a mixing bowl and rub in the yeast. Scoop the ferment into the bowl, then add the water, oil, and salt, mixing well until all combined (use one hand to mix and hold the bowl with the other). Once the dough is no longer sticking to the bowl, transfer it to your counter with the help of the rounded end of your scraper, and work it following the method on page 24. (If you prefer to use a mixer, combine the ingredients as above, mixing for another 4–5 minutes on the second speed until the dough is light, supple, and elastic.) Remove the dough from the bowl, transfer to a lightly oiled surface, and mold into a ball (page 25).

• Lightly oil a bowl either with avocado or olive oil, place the dough in it, and let rest for 1¹/₂ hours, covered with a lintfree dishtowel, until it has risen and feels bubbly and light.

• Flour your work surface generously with white flour or cornmeal, and with the help of the rounded end of your scraper, turn the dough out in one piece. Flour the top. Press the dough lightly and gently, dimpling it slightly with your fingers. Divide the dough into four roughly equal strips, and fold into three. Do this by folding one side of your flattened dough into the middle and press it down and seal. Bring the other side over to the middle and again press down to seal. Finally fold in half lengthwise and seal the edges.

• Place the pieces of dough onto well-floured lintfree dishtowels. Cover with another towel and let rise for 30–45 minutes.

• Flour a baking tray or wooden peel, pick up one ciabatta at a time, turn it over, stretch it lengthwise a little at the same time, and lay it on the peel or tray. (This stretch is what gives the bread its characteristic "slipper" shape.) Spray the inside of your oven with a water spray and then quickly slide the ciabatta onto the baking stone or tray. Turn down the heat to 435ºF (220°C) and bake for 18–20 minutes until light brown.

Part-baking for the freezer: The bread can be part-baked for 15 minutes and then cooled, wrapped well in freezer bags, and frozen. To use them, bake from frozen for 12 minutes at 400ºF (200°C).

Variation: Olive Ciabatta
Add 7 ounces purple Kalamata or green, pitted and quartered olives (about 1 1/2 cups) during the last few minutes of working the dough.

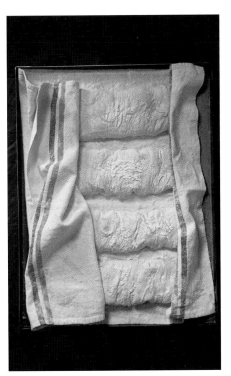

3. Brown Dough

Brown: dusky; like wood or ea

Many of the breads in this chapter have an autumnal, even Christmasy feel, because there is something earthy about brown bread which lends itself to fruit and spice and feels warming and cheering on a cold winter's day. Mostly I use a combination of white flour and whole-wheat, which gives a lighter loaf than pure whole-wheat and, though I have included one for 100% whole-wheat, it is still lighter than most because it uses a ferment (page 14). Although the way of working the brown dough is the same as for the previous two chapters, don't worry if it seems slightly heavier.

10^1/$_2$ ounces Whole-wheat bread flour (about 2^1/$_3$ cups)

7 ounces White bread flour (about 1^1/$_2$ cups)

^{1}/$_3$ ounce Fresh yeast preferably or ^{1}/$_4$-oz. (7g) envelope active dry yeast (1^1/$_2$ teaspoons)

^{1}/$_3$ ounce Salt (about 2 teaspoons fine-grain)

12^1/$_2$ ounces Water (13fl. oz. in a glass measuring cup—just over 1^1/$_2$ cups)

Preheat your oven to 475°F (250°C). Mix the two flours together and rub in the yeast, using your fingertips as if making a crumble. Add the salt and water, then continue according to the method on pages 22-25.

honey &
lavender
loaf

raisin,
hazeln
& sha
bread

poppy
seed s

apricot &
oat bread

sesam
braid

brown

eed
d

pecan &
cranberry
bread

iseed
vn
d

100%
whole-
wheat
bread

amom
une
d

apricot & oat bread

I like this bread for breakfast—it's a little bit like muesli in bread form—but it's equally good toasted with cheese. The apricots (I use organic ones, with no artificial preservatives) give it a slight sweetness and the oats a little crunchiness.

Quantity:	4 small or 2 large loaves	**1 Batch**	Brown dough (page 93)
Preparation:	20 minutes	**7 ounces**	Dried apricots (preferably organic), roughly chopped (about 1 cup)
Resting:	70 minutes	**3 ounces**	Oats (about 3/4 cup)
2nd Rising:	1 hour		
Baking:	15 minutes baking for the small or 25 minutes for the large		

To prepare

Make the dough as explained on page 22 but add the apricots at the end of working it by hand or mixing in a mixer and continue working/mixing until the apricots are distributed evenly. Form the dough into a ball (page 25), place in a lightly floured bowl, cover with a lintfree dishtowel and let it rest for 1 hour.

To make

• With the help of the rounded end of your scraper, turn the dough out onto a lightly floured counter and divide it into two or four pieces depending on the size of loaf you want. Shape into balls again, cover with a lintfree dishtowel, and let it rest for 10 minutes.

• Mold each ball into a loaf (page 31). Place the oats on a plate. Brush the tops and sides of each loaf with a little water then roll it in the oats until they generously coat the loaf. Place the loaves on a cookie sheet with a lightly floured lintfree dishtowel, pleated in between the loaves so they don't touch as they rise.

• With a razor blade or sharp knife, make a few diagonal cuts along the top of each loaf with a depth of at least 2 inches (5mm), then let them rise for 1 hour or until the loaves have nearly doubled in volume.

• Open the preheated oven and mist the inside with a water spray, then quickly slide the loaves onto the baking stone or tray and close the door. Turn down the heat to 425°F (220°C) and bake for 15 minutes for the small loaves or about 25 minutes for the large ones. Once baked, the loaves should sound hollow when tapped on the bottom with your finger. Cool on a wire rack.

honey & lavender loaf

Just a teaspoon of lavender gives the most extraordinary flavor, but I know not everyone likes it. If you don't, then forget this recipe! Personally I think this loaf is just beautiful toasted with soft goat cheese. We love lavender so much we grow it in the garden, pick it at the end of the summer, and then spend a somewhat tedious, if fragrant, evening taking off the heads and spreading them out to dry on baking trays. Once they are dry, we put them into a plastic container which will keep us in lavender until it is in season again. If you have some lavender honey, you could use that as well—otherwise use another good-quality honey, preferably organic.

Quantity:	1 large loaf
Preparation:	20 minutes
Resting:	1¹/₂ hours
2nd Rising:	1–1¹/₂ hours
Baking:	30–40 minutes

1 Batch Brown dough (page 93)

1 Heaped teaspoon Lavender flowers (fresh/dried)

1 ounce Good-quality runny honey or lavender honey (about 1¹/₂ tablespoons)

To prepare

Make the dough following the method on pages 22–25 but add the lavender at the same time as the flour, and the honey along with the salt. Shape the dough into a ball (page 25), place in a lightly floured bowl, cover with a lintfree dishtowel and let it rest for 45 minutes.

To make

• With the help of your plastic scraper, turn the dough out onto your counter, then reshape it into a ball, put back into the bowl, cover, and let rest for 45 minutes more.

• Turn the dough out onto the counter and press it down gently. Shape it into a square by drawing the four "corners" into the center. Flour the top of the loaf. Flour a lintfree dishtowel and place the loaf onto it, folded-side-down. Cover with another towel and let it rise for 1–1¹/₂ hours until it has nearly doubled in volume.

• Place the loaf (folded-side-down) on a wooden peel or upside-down baking tray and mark a double cross shape on the top of the loaf with a razor blade or sharp knife. Mist the inside of the preheated oven with a water spray and quickly slide the loaf onto the baking stone or tray. Turn down the heat to 425°F (220°C) and bake for 10 minutes, then turn down again to 400°F (200°C) and bake for 20–30 minutes more. Once baked the loaf should sound hollow if tapped on the bottom with your finger. You will need to keep testing it, as with a large loaf such as this it's difficult to be absolutely accurate about timing.

cardamom & prune bread

I first tried using cardamom in a Danish-style pastry I happened to be experimenting with. I knew it was a spice that worked well with fruit, so I added some prunes, but still I felt there was something missing. So, I cast my mind back to my days in Brittany, when we used to make Far Breton, a kind of batter cake with prunes and good dark rum. When I tried adding the rum, the flavors really brought the bread alive, transforming it into something warm and earthy and Christmasy.

Quantity:	2 loaves	
Preparation:	30 minutes	
Resting:	1³/₄ hours	
2nd Rising:	1 hour	
Baking:	25–30 minutes	

1 Batch Brown dough (page 93)
4 ounces Pitted prunes (about ³/₄ cup)
1/4 cup Rum
¹/₄ teaspoon Freshly ground cardamom

To prepare

Soak the prunes in the rum for at least 1 hour, or overnight if possible.

Make the dough following the method on page 22, but increase the yeast quantity to 15g to counteract the weight of the fruit. Add the cardamom along with the flour, and add the prunes towards the end of working the dough by hand or mixing in a mixer. Continue working/mixing until everything is evenly distributed. Shape the dough into a ball (page 25), place in a bowl, cover with a lintfree dishtowel and let it rest for 1 hour.

To make

• With the help of the rounded end of your scraper, turn out the dough onto a lightly floured counter and reshape into a ball, put back in the bowl, cover with a lintfree dishtowel and let it rest for 45 minutes more.

• Again using the rounded end of your scraper, turn out the dough onto a lightly floured counter and divide in half. Mold each half into a loaf (page 31). Place on a lightly floured lintfree dishtowel on a shallow-edged or upside-down baking tray. Flour the top of the loaves and then, with a razor blade or sharp knife, make four diagonal cuts, to a depth of 2 inches (5mm), fanning out on either side of the loaf. Cover with a lintfree dishtowel and let rise for 1 hour, until they have nearly doubled in volume.

• Open the preheated oven and mist with a water spray. Slide the loaves onto the baking stone or tray in the oven. Turn down the heat to 425°F (220°C) and bake for 25–30 minutes. Once baked, the loaves should sound hollow when tapped on the bottom. Remove from the oven and cool on a wire rack.

Top to bottom: cardamom & prune bread; apricot & oat bread; raisin, hazelnut & shallot bread; pecan & cranberry bread; seaweed bread

seaweed bread

If you ask people to identify the flavor of this bread, I doubt if they would be able to recognize it as seaweed —but everyone I have made this for has loved it. I used to do something similar in Brittany using local seaweed but here I find Japanese wakame works really well. Because of its affinity with the sea, it is fantastic with seafood, especially fresh oysters.

Quantity:	1 loaf
Preparation:	30 minutes
Resting:	1³/₄ hours
2nd Rising:	1 hour
Baking:	45 minutes

9 ounces White bread flour (about 2 cups)

9 ounces Whole-wheat flour (about 2 cups)

¹/₃ ounce Fresh yeast preferably or ¹/₄-oz. (7g) envelope active dry yeast (1¹/₂ teaspoons)

¹/₃ ounce Salt (about 2 teaspoons fine-grain)

12 ounces Water (13 fl. oz. in glass measuring cup)

¹/₃ ounce (10g) Dehydrated wakame seaweed (this should give you about 2 ounces (50g) rehydrated seaweed), or use nori seaweed (about 3 sheets) but don't soak it first

To prepare

Soak the wakame seaweed in water, according to the instructions on the pack, until soft. Mix the two flours and rub in the yeast, add the salt and then the water and make the dough following the method on pages 22–25. Add the seaweed at the end of working by hand or mixing in the mixer and continue working/mixing until it is evenly distributed through the dough. Shape the dough into a ball (page 25), place it in a lightly floured bowl, cover with a lintfree dishtowel and let it rest for 1 hour. Preheat the oven to 475°F.

To make

• With the help of the rounded end of your scraper, turn the dough out of the bowl and reshape into a ball, place it back in the bowl, cover with a lintfree dishtowel and let it rest for 45 minutes more.

• Turn the dough out onto a lightly floured counter and mold it into a loaf shape (page 31). Let it rise for 1 hour on a well-floured lintfree dishtowel, seam-side-up.

• Turn the loaf over and place on a wooden peel or flat-edged baking tray. With a razor or sharp knife, make three cuts on either side fanning out from the middle, along the top of the bread. Mist the inside of your preheated oven with a water spray and then slide the loaf onto the hot stone or upturned tray. Bake for about 45 minutes until well colored. The loaf should sound hollow when tapped on the bottom with your finger. Remove from the oven and cool on a wire rack.

sesame plaits

These are tiny braided rolls which are good fun to make.

Quantity:	12 braids	**1 Batch** Brown dough (page 93) rested for 1 hour
Preparation:	45 minutes	**Heaped 1/3 cup** Sesame seeds
Resting:	65 minutes	
2nd Rising:	45 minutes	
Baking:	12–15 minutes	

To make

• Turn the rested dough out with the help of the rounded end of your scraper. With the flat edge, divide it into twelve equal pieces and roll them into balls (page 28). Cover with a lintfree dishtowel and let it rest for 5 minutes.

• Lightly flour the counter. Take one of the balls and flatten it to form a disc. Fold in two of the sides to the center to form a rough rectangle, then turn it over so the folds are underneath. Using a sharp-bladed knife, make two parallel cuts straight through the dough starting just short of one end and going all the way down to the other, so that you end up with three strands joined together at one end by a strip of dough.

• Braid the strands by passing each one of the outer strands over the middle one in turn. Repeat until you reach the ends, and seal by rolling each end of the braid until pointed. Repeat with the other eleven balls.

• Put the sesame seeds on a plate. Brush the tops of the rolls with a little water and dip (tops only) into the seeds. Place on a baking tray, cover with a lintfree dishtowel, and let them rise in a warm, draft-free place for 45 minutes or until they have nearly doubled in volume.

• Put into the preheated oven. Using a water spray, mist the inside of the oven just before you close the door. Turn down the heat to 425°F (220°C) and bake for 12–15 minutes.

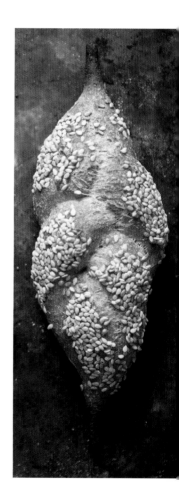

brown rolls

These are the whole-wheat equivalent of the Lemon Rolls in chapter 1, but shaped more simply.

Quantity:	12 rolls	**1 Batch** Brown dough (page 93) rested for 1 hour	
Preparation:	30 minutes		
Resting:	65 minutes		
2nd Rising:	45 minutes		
Baking:	10 minutes		

To make

• Turn the dough out onto a lightly floured counter with the help of the rounded end of your scraper. Divide it into 12 equal pieces and mold each one into a ball (page 28). Place them on a baking tray, cover with a lintfree dishtowel and let rest on your counter for 5 minutes.

• After resting, shape into balls again, roll a little into an oval shape, and place on a second baking tray, again leaving enough space for the rolls to rise without touching. Cover with a lintfree dishtowel.

• Leave the rolls in a draft-free place to rise for 45 minutes until they have nearly doubled in volume.

• Using a razor blade or sharp knife, make one long cut lengthwise, from one tip to the other. Open the preheated oven and mist with a water spray. Quickly put the rolls in the oven, turn down the heat to 450°F (230°C) and bake for 10 minutes. Cool on a wire rack.

poppy seed stars

These look really pretty on a bread board alongside other shapes or styles of rolls and breadsticks.

Quantity:	12 stars	**1 Batch** Brown dough (page 93) rested for 1 hour
Preparation:	45 minutes	**2 ounces** Poppy seeds (about 5 tablespoons)
Resting:	65 minutes	
2nd Rising:	45 minutes	
Baking:	10–12 minutes	

To make

• With the rounded end of your scraper, turn out the dough. Divide it into 12 pieces (about 2¹/₂ ounces each) and roll them into balls (page 28), cover them with a lintfree dishtowel and rest for 5 minutes.

• Scatter the poppy seeds on a plate and fill a shallow bowl with water. Flatten one of the rolls with the palm of your hand, dip the top into the water, then immediately into the seeds and press them in with your hand. Place on a lightly floured counter, seed-side-up, and flatten a little with your hand. Using the short end of a clean credit card, make a diagonal cut across the center of the dough—the cut shouldn't reach the edges of the roll but should go all the way through it to the work surface. Then make two other diagonal cuts that intersect the first one equally, so that the three cuts form a star shape. Carefully push the roll from underneath with your fingertips, and turn it inside out, so that the points of the star push upwards and outwards, resulting in the points being on the outside. Place the stars on a baking tray, seed-side-up, cover with a lintfree dishtowel and let rise for about 45 minutes until the stars have nearly doubled in volume.

• Put them in the preheated oven, mist the inside with a water spray, and bake them for 10–12 minutes.

multiseed brown bread

This is a very earthy, crunchy but simple bread, for which I use a multigrain flour.

Quantity:	2 loaves
Preparation:	15 minutes
Resting:	70 minutes
2nd Rising:	1 hour
Baking:	15–20 minutes

7 ounces Whole-wheat bread flour (about 1^1/$_2$ cups)

6 ounces White bread flour

4^1/$_2$ ounces Multigrain flour (about 1 cup), plus some more for topping

^{1}/$_3$ ounce Fresh yeast preferably or ^{1}/$_4$-oz. (7g) envelope active dry yeast (1^1/$_2$ teaspoons)

^{1}/$_3$ ounce Salt (about 2 teaspoons fine-grain)

12 ounces Water (13 fl. oz. in glass measuring cup)

A little butter for greasing

To prepare

Grease 2 x 1-pound, 8-8^1/$_2$ inches (20–22cm) long pans with a little butter. Preheat the oven to 475°F. Mix the three flours together and rub in the yeast, using your fingertips as if making a crumble. Add the salt and water, then continue according to the method on pages 22–25. Mold the dough into a ball (page 25), place in a lightly floured bowl, cover with a lintfree dishtowel and let rest for 1 hour.

To make

• With the help of the rounded end of your scraper, turn the dough out onto a counter and divide it into two equal pieces. Form each into a ball, cover with a lintfree dishtowel and let it rest for 10 minutes more.

• Mold each ball into a loaf (page 31) but, before putting the loaves into the pans, brush the tops with a little water and roll them in some more multigrain flour. Cover with another lintfree dishtowel and let rise for about 1 hour or until the loaves have nearly doubled in volume.

• Open the preheated oven and mist the inside with a water spray. Quickly place the pans on the baking stone or tray in the oven and close the door. Bake the loaves for 15–20 minutes. Remove and cool on a wire rack.

raisin, hazelnut, & shallot bread

This is lovely toasted with some cheese and homemade chutney, or ham and some good mustard.

Quantity: 2 loaves
Preparation: 45 minutes
Resting: 1 1/2 hours
2nd Rising: 1–1 1/4 hours
Baking: 30 minutes

1 Batch Brown dough (page 93)
1 teaspoon Good-quality runny honey (preferably organic)

A little Oil
A pat of Butter
3 ounces Shallots, sliced (about 3/4 cup)
3 ounces Hazelnuts, crushed (about 3/4 cup)
3 ounces Raisins (about 1/3 cup)

To make

• Put the oil and pat of butter into a really hot frying pan. Add the shallots and stir from time to time until they are soft and brown. Add the crushed hazelnuts, stir and cook over medium heat for 1 minute, then add the raisins, stir again, and cook for another 30 seconds. Remove from the heat and transfer to a plate to cool.

• Make the dough following the method on pages 22–25, adding the honey along with the salt and water. Towards the end of working by hand or mixing in a mixer, add the shallot mixture and continue working/mixing until it's evenly distributed. Form the dough into a ball (page 25), put it into a lightly floured bowl, cover with a lintfree dishtowel and let it rest for 45 minutes. Turn the dough out onto the counter and fold it over on itself a few times. Reshape it into a ball, put it back into the bowl, cover, and let it rest for another 45 minutes.

• Lightly flour your counter. Divide the dough into two equal pieces and mold each one into a loaf (page 31). Lightly flour a lintfree dishtowel with whole-wheat flour and lay it on a tray. Lift the center of the tea towel gently to form a ridge and place one loaf (smooth-side-down) on each side of the ridge. Cover with another lintfree dishtowel and let rise for 1-1 1/4 hours or until the loaves have nearly doubled in volume.

• Turn the loaves over and place on a peel or flat-edged cookie sheet. With a razor blade or sharp knife, make one long cut the length of the top of each bread, to a depth of about 2 inches (5mm). Mist the inside of your oven with a water spray and then slide the loaves onto the baking stone or tray. Bake them for about 30 minutes until well colored. The loaves should sound hollow when tapped on the bottom with your finger. Remove from the oven and cool on a wire rack.

pecan & cranberry bread

I was thinking about Christmas and cranberries when I first made this, and because there happened to be some pecans around I added those, too. All the flavors just seemed to work really happily with the whole-wheat flour, and I discovered that the bread goes well with Stilton.

Quantity:	1 large or 2 small loaves	**1 Batch** Brown dough (page 93)	
Preparation:	20 minutes	**3¹/₂ ounces** Shelled pecans (about 1 cup)	
Resting:	65 minutes	**3¹/₂ ounces** Dried cranberries (about 1 cup)	
2nd Rising:	1 hour	**Zest of 1** Large orange	
Baking:	20 minutes baking for small loaves or 40 minutes for a large loaf		

To prepare

Crush the pecans—I do this with the end of a rolling pin or you could use a pestle and mortar.
Mix the pecans, cranberries, and orange zest.
Make the brown dough following the method on pages 22-25, but add the pecan and cranberry mix towards the end of working by hand or mixing in the mixer, and ensure the mix is evenly distributed. Form the dough into a ball (page 25) and place in a lightly floured bowl covered with a lintfree dishtowel to rest for 1 hour.

To make

• Turn the dough out onto a well floured counter and divide in half if you want to make two smaller loaves. Form into a ball or balls and let rest for another 5 minutes.

• Mold again into a tight ball (or two) and place, smooth-side-down, in a floured wicker bread-raising basket (if you have one) or a bowl lined with a floured lintfree dishtowel. Cover with another dishtowel and let rise for about 1 hour until the dough has nearly doubled in volume.

• Turn the dough out of the bowl or basket and place on a peel or flat-edged cookie sheet. Cut a cross into the top of the loaf (loaves) with a razor blade or sharp knife. Open the preheated oven and mist the inside with a water spray. Quickly slide the loaf (or loaves) onto the baking stone or tray and close the door. Bake small loaves at 425°F (220°C) for the first 5 minutes then turn the oven down to 400°F (200°C) for the remaining 15 minutes. For a large loaf, bake for 5 minutes at 425°F (220°C), then another 30–35 minutes at 400°F (200°C). Remove from the oven and cool on a wire rack.

100% whole-wheat bread

This is heavier, but not as heavy as many breads made only with whole-wheat flour, because it is made with a "poolish", a style of ferment which was introduced into France by Polish bakers and which packs the bread with flavor and character, and helps lighten it.

Quantity: 2 loaves
Preparation: 15 minutes
Resting: 3–5 hours for the poolish
                  30 minutes for the bread
Proving: 1 hour
Baking: 30–35 minutes

For the poolish ferment:
5g Fresh yeast
9 ounces Tepid water (just over a cup)
9 ounces Whole-wheat flour (about 2 cups)

9 ounces Whole-wheat flour (about 2 cups)
5g Fresh Yeast
1/3 ounce Salt (about 2 teaspoons fine-grain)
3 ounces Water (about 1/3 cup)
A little butter for greasing

To prepare

Butter 2 x 1-pound, 8-8^{1}/$_{2}$-inch (20–22cm long) loaf pans. Preheat the oven to 475°F (250°C).
To make the poolish, whisk the yeast into the water until it has completely dissolved, then add the flour and whisk to obtain a batter. Cover with a lintfree dishtowel and let rest for at least 3 hours, but no longer than 5, by which time it should have around doubled in volume—it is ready when it has formed into a dome and then slightly flattened out—at this point you need to use it quickly, otherwise it will start to collapse.
Add the rest of the ingredients to the poolish (rub the yest into the dough first), mix well using your scraper, and work by hand following the method on page 24, until the dough is supple and no longer sticks to your hand or the counter. Shape the dough into a ball and put into a lightly floured bowl, covered with a lintfree dishtowel, and let it rest for 15 minutes.

To make

• With the help of the rounded edge of your scraper, turn the dough out onto the counter and divide it into two. Form each into a ball again, cover with a lintfree dishtowel and let rest for another 15 minutes.

• Mold the two pieces of dough into tight loaves (page 31) and place in the greased loaf pans. Cover with a lintfree dishtowel and let rise for about 1 hour until they have nearly doubled in volume.

• Dust the tops of the loaves with a little whole-wheat flour. Put them into the preheated oven. With a water spray mist the inside of the oven just before you close the door. Bake them for 30–35 minutes until the bottom sounds hollow when you tap it. Remove from the oven and cool on a wire rack.

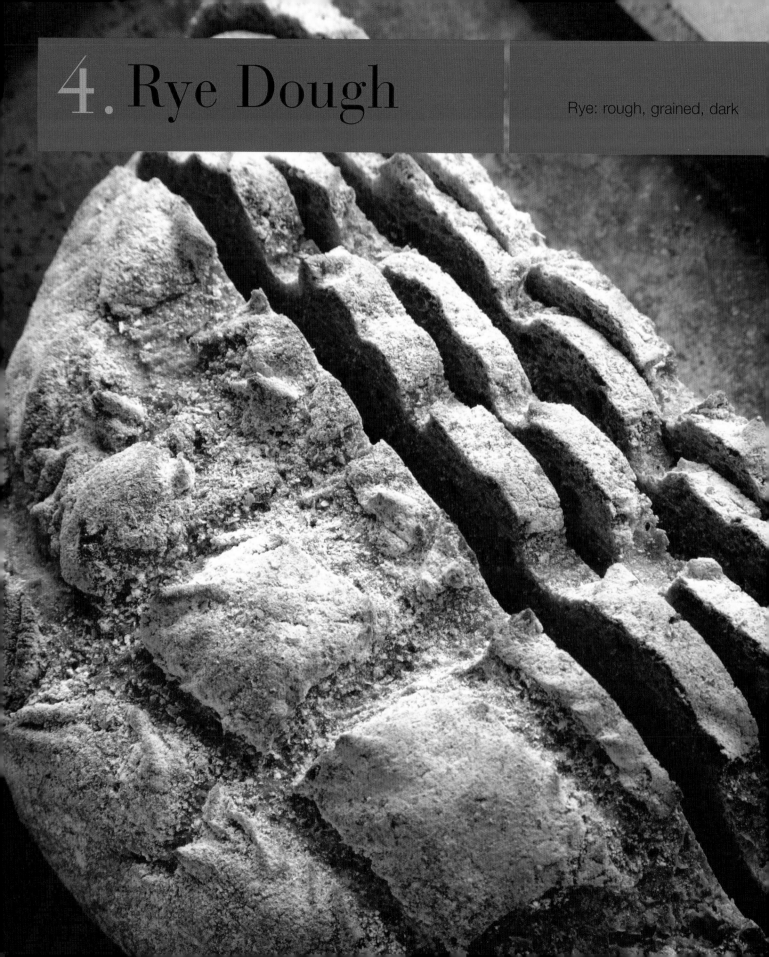

4. Rye Dough

Most people associate rye bread with dark, heavy Scandinavian and Germanic-style breads such as pumpernickel. However, when you blend white bread flour with the rye flour, it lifts and lightens the texture, giving a really tasty, rustic bread that offers a wonderful base for ingredients like olives, fruit, nuts, and spices. If you like your rye bread darker still, then just increase the ratio of rye flour to white, or if you prefer it lighter, you can increase the percentage of white flour.

14 ounces White bread flour (about 3 cups)
3¹/₂ ounces Dark rye flour (about ³/₄ cup)
¹/₃ ounce Fresh yeast preferably or ¹/₄-oz. (7g) envelope active dry yeast (1¹/₂ teaspoons)
¹/₃ ounce Salt (about 2 teaspoons fine-grain)
12¹/₂ ounces Water (13fl. oz. in a glass measuring cup—just over 1¹/₂ cups)

Preheat the oven to 250ºC. Mix the two flours together and rub in the yeast, using your fingertips as if making a crumble. Add the salt and water, then continue according to the method on pages 22–25.

dark rye
bread
poolish
fermen

somerset
cider bread

rye,
carawa
raisin b

pain de
campagne

bread

walnut
bread

anise &
guinness
bread

ked
on & red
n bread

walnut bread

I sometimes make this with a combination of walnuts and dates (while prunes have a natural affinity with whole-wheat bread, dates are perfect with rye—raisins are good, too). If you are going to use fruit, reduce the quantity of walnuts to 5 ounces (1¹/₃ cups), and add 4 ounces (¹/₂ cup) chopped dates or raisins.

Quantity:	2 rings	**1 Batch** Rye dough (page 117)
Preparation:	30 minutes	**2 cups** Shelled walnuts, crushed using a rolling pin
Resting:	65 minutes	or pestle and mortar (when broken unevenly they
2nd Rising:	1 hour	release their oil into the dough more easily)
Baking:	20 minutes	Flour for dusting

To make

• Make the dough following the method on pages 22–25, adding the walnuts at the end of working by hand or mixing in the mixer and continue working/mixing until they are evenly distributed. Shape the dough into a ball (page 25), put it into a lightly floured bowl, cover with a lintfree dishtowel and let rest for 1 hour. With the help of the rounded end of your scraper, turn out the dough onto a lightly floured counter and divide into two. Shape each piece into a ball, cover with a lintfree dishtowel and rest for another 5 minutes, then re-mold the dough into a tight ball. Press the end of your rolling pin into the center of each ball until you reach the counter and have made a hole. Flour your hands and then open up the hole to form a ring—the hole should be at least the size of a fist to prevent it from closing up as the dough rises. Lightly flour a lintfree dishtowel and place the bread rings on top. Cover with another dishtowel and let rise for about 1 hour until the rings have nearly doubled in volume. Transfer to a peel or flat-edged cookie sheet and with a razor or sharp knife, make three cuts at equal points around the ring. Open the preheated oven and mist with a water spray. Quickly slide the rings onto the baking stone, turn down the heat to 425°F (220°C), and bake for 5 minutes, then turn down to 400°F (200°C) and bake for another 15 minutes. Remove and cool on a wire rack.

olive bread

This bread is inspired by the beautiful little pain de campagne-style loaves you find, filled with dark olive paste, in the markets of Provence—stunning.

Quantity:	3 loaves	
Preparation:	40 minutes	
Resting:	1 hour	
2nd Rising:	1 hour	
Baking:	18–20 minutes	

1 Batch Rye dough (page 117) rested for 1 hour
7 ounces Olive paste (about 1 cup)
Flour for dusting

To make

• With the help of the rounded end of your scraper, turn the dough out onto a lightly floured counter and divide it into three pieces. Take one of the pieces and flatten it with the palm of your hand into a rough rectangular shape. Spread about 2 tablespoons of the paste over the dough. Then fold and form into a loaf (page 31). Repeat with the other two pieces.

• Place the loaves (seam-side-down) onto a lightly floured lintfree dishtowel, flour the top of the loaves, and pull the towel into low ridges in between the loaves so that they do not end up touching as they rise. Cover with a second dishtowel and let rise for 1 hour or until the loaves have nearly doubled in volume.

• Transfer the loaves to a peel or flat-edged cookie sheet and make a single cut down the middle of each loaf with a razor blade or sharp knife. Open the preheated oven and mist the inside with a water spray, then quickly slide the loaves onto the preheated baking stone or tray and close the door. Bake them for 18–20 minutes. The loaves should sound hollow when tapped on the bottom with your finger. Cool on a wire rack.

olive paste

Drain and remove the pits from 7 ounces (about 1 1/2 cups) Picholine (Provençal) olives (or similar). Put into a food processor with 2 teaspoons herbes de Provence and 2 tablespoons extra-virgin olive oil and blitz until you have a coarse paste. You can store this in an airtight container in the fridge for a few days. Alternatively you can freeze the paste for several weeks, defrost it at room temperature, and add a few drops of lemon juice to refresh it when you need it. This will make 7 ounces.

rye, caraway & raisin bread

Rye and caraway are a classic combination, and the raisins just add a sweetness which works really well with cheese, especially blue cheese. Caraway is a favorite of mine—I love the aroma of the seeds when the bread is baking—but you can reduce the quantity if you are less partial to it.

Quantity:	2 loaves	**1 Batch** Rye dough (page 117)
Preparation:	20 minutes	**9 ounces** Raisins or golden raisins (about 1¹/₃ cups)
Resting:	70 minutes	**1 teaspoon** Caraway seeds
2nd Rising:	1 hour	Flour for dusting
Baking:	30 minutes	

To prepare
Mix the fruit and caraway seeds together.
Make the dough following the method on pages 22–25, adding the fruit and caraway shortly before the end of working by hand or mixing in the mixer. Continue working/mixing until they are evenly distributed. Shape the dough into a ball (page 25), place in a bowl, cover with a lintfree dishtowel and let rest for 1 hour.

To make
• With the help of the rounded end of the scraper, turn out the dough onto a lightly floured counter and divide into two. Mold each into a ball, cover with a lintfree dishtowel, and leave on the counter to rest for 10 minutes.

• Mold each ball into a tight loaf shape of about 20cm (8-inch) length (page 31). Lightly flour a lintfree dishtowel and place the loaves onto it, seam-side-up, making a pleat in the towel in between each one, so that they do not touch as they rise. Cover with another lintfree dishtowel and let rise for 1 hour until they have nearly doubled in volume.

• Turn the loaves over and transfer to a peel or flat-edged baking tray and cut a leaf pattern (one cut down the center, with four cuts fanning out on each side) in the top with a razor or sharp knife. Mist the inside of the preheated oven with a water spray. Slide the loaves onto the baking stone or tray and quickly close the door. Turn the heat down to 425°F (220°C) and bake for 30 minutes. The loaves sound hollow when tapped on the bottom. Remove and cool on a wire rack.

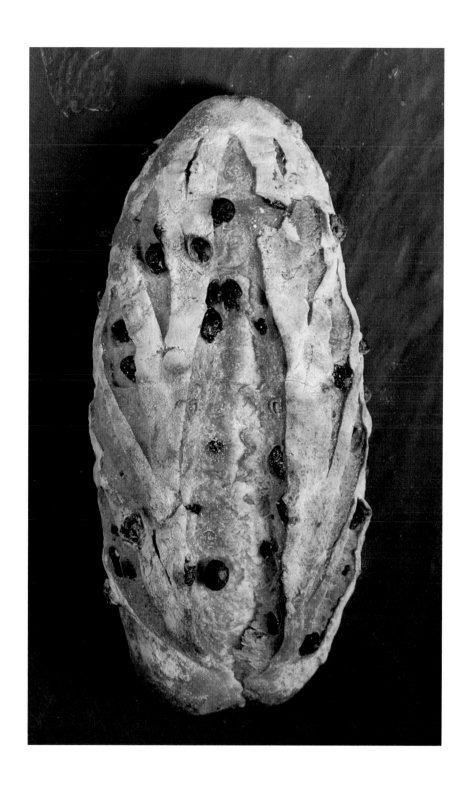

smoked bacon & red onion bread

Smoked bacon and red onion are a great combination, which make a beautiful loaf to slice for sandwiches, or to serve with something like a chicken liver salad. Make sure you use good bacon, preferably dry-cured in the traditional fashion. The balsamic vinegar is only a dash to deglaze the pan, so it doesn't need to be the best quality—or you could use a tablespoon of red wine or red wine vinegar instead.

Quantity:	4 small loaves
Preparation:	30 minutes
Resting:	70 minutes
2nd Rising:	1 1/4 hours
Baking:	20 minutes

1 Batch Rye dough (page 117)
1 tablespoon Olive oil
8 Thick slices Smoked, dry, cured bacon, snipped into strips
1 Large Red onion, finely sliced
1 tablespoon Balsamic vinegar
Flour for dusting

To make

• Preheat the oven to 250°C. Heat the oil in a frying pan and fry the bacon over medium heat for a couple of minutes until it starts to brown and crisp, then add the onion and cook for another couple of minutes. Deglaze the pan by pouring in the vinegar and stirring well over the heat for another minute or so, scraping all the bits of bacon from the bottom. Transfer the bacon, onion, and juices into a dish to cool.

• Make the dough according to the method on pages 22–25, adding the bacon mixture towards the end of working the dough by hand or mixing in a mixer and continue to work/mix until it is evenly distributed. Form the dough into a ball (page 25), put into a lightly floured bowl, cover with a dishtowel, and let rest for 1 hour.

• With the help of the rounded end of your scraper, turn the dough out onto a lightly floured counter and divide it into four roughly equal pieces. Mold each into a ball, cover with a lintfree dishtowel and leave on the counter to rest for another 10 minutes. Reshape each of the pieces into a tight ball again. Lightly flour a lintfree dishtowel (or two) and place the balls, smooth-side-up, on top. Cover with another dishtowel (or towels) and let rise for about 1 1/4 hours until they have nearly doubled in volume.

• Transfer to a peel or flat-edged cookie sheet and make a circular cut on the top of each loaf with a razor or sharp knife. Mist your preheated oven with a water spray, quickly slide the loaves onto the baking stone or tray, and bake at 425°F (220°C) for 5 minutes, then turn down the heat to 375°F (190°C) and bake for another 15 minutes. The loaf should sound hollow if tapped on the bottom. Cool on a wire rack.

somerset cider bread

This was a bread I made to celebrate our move to Bath to set up my cookery school. Adding cider, or ale lends the bread a real "country," rustic note, while the flavor is deepened by the addition of some previously made rye dough, which has been left to ferment. This is a bread that is fabulous with some cured ham or a proper, traditional cheddar. In this bread, I suggest you make a larger quantity of dough, as I feel the ferment works better with more bulk.

Quantity:	4 loaves
Preparation:	20 minutes
Resting:	4–6 hours for the ferment
	1½ hours for the dough
2nd Rising:	1¼–1½ hours
Baking:	45 minutes

½ Batch Rye dough (page 117) left to ferment for 4–6 hours

⅓ ounce Fresh yeast preferably or ¼-oz. (7g) envelope active dry yeast (1½ teaspoons)

26½ ounces White bread flour (about 5¾ cups)

9 ounces Dark rye flour (about 2 cups)

⅔ ounce Salt (about 4 teaspoons fine-grain)

16 ounces Good-quality dry cider (about 17f fl. oz. in glass measuring cup)

5½ ounces Water (about ¾ cup)

Flour for dusting

To make

• Use your scraper to scoop the ferment from its container into your bowl, all in one piece, and add the rest of your ingredients. Make the dough following the method on pages 22–25. Shape the dough into a ball, put it into a lightly floured bowl, cover with a lintfree dishtowel and let it rest for 45 minutes.

• With the help of the rounded end of your plastic scraper, turn the dough onto a lightly floured work surface and reshape into a ball, place it back into the bowl, cover with a tea towel and leave to rest for 45 minutes.

• Using the scraper again, turn the dough out onto your lightly floured counter and divide it into four equal pieces. Lightly flour a couple of lintfree dishtowels. Mold the balls of dough into loaves (page 31) and place two on top of each towel, making a fold in the fabric between them to stop them touching when they rise. Cover with a dishtowel and let them rise for 1¼–1½ hours, or until they have nearly doubled in volume.

• Turn the loaves over, place on a peel or flat-edged cookie sheet and make 1 cut lengthwise along the top of the loaves with a razor blade or sharp knife. Mist the inside of your preheated oven with a water spray and slide the loaves onto the baking stone/tray. Bake for 10 minutes, then turn down the heat to 400°F (200°C) and bake for 35 minutes until well colored. The loaves should sound hollow when tapped on the bottom. Remove and cool on a wire rack.

anise & guinness bread

I love anise—particularly in pastis, and since I'm told that "Black Velvet" can be made either with Champagne or pastis and Guinness, this seemed to me to be the perfect combination of flavors. It's wonderful served, Irish style, with seafood, especially oysters, and a drop more Guinness—cold, and in a glass, this time.

Quantity: 3 loaves
Preparation: 30 minutes
Resting: 3 hours 35 minutes for the bread
2nd Rising: 1 1/2 hours
Baking: 30 minutes

1 ounce Fresh yeast (preferably) or 1/3 ounce active dry yeast (2 teaspoons)
25 ounces Guinness, at room temperature (just under 27 fl. oz. in glass measuring cup)
9 ounces Dark rye flour (about 2 cups)
26 1/2 ounces White bread flour (about 5 3/4 cups)
2/3 ounce Salt (about 4 teaspoons fine-grain)
1 tablespoon Pastis (or other anise liqueur)
Flour for dusting

To make

• Whisk the yeast into the Guinness in a large mixing bowl until it has completely dissolved, then add the rye flour and 3 cups of the white flour and whisk to obtain a thick batter. Cover with a lintfree dishtowel and let rest for 2 hours. Preheat the oven to 475°F (250°C).

• Add the rest of the ingredients to the batter, mix well, and continue making the dough following the method on page 22, until the dough is supple and elastic, and no longer sticks to your hands. Shape into a ball (page 25), and put into a lightly floured bowl, cover with a lintfree dishtowel and let it rest for 45 minutes.

• With the help of the rounded end of your scraper, turn the dough out onto a lightly floured counter and reshape into a ball, place back in the bowl, cover with a towel and let rest for another 45 minutes. Again turn the dough out and divide it into three equal pieces. Reshape each into a ball, and leave on the counter, covered with a towel, to rest for another 5 minutes. Lay some lintfree dishtowels on a cookie sheet and lightly flour them. Mold the balls into loaves (page 31), and place them on the dishtowels, leaving a good space in between them. Cover and let them rise for 1 1/2 hours, or until they have nearly doubled in volume.

• Place the loaves on a peel or flat-edged cookie sheet, and make two diagonal cuts on top of the loaf with a razor blade or sharp knife. Mist the inside of your preheated oven with a water spray and slide the loaves onto the baking stone/tray. Bake them for 5 minutes, reduce the heat to 425°F (220°C) and bake for another 25 minutes until they are a rich dark color. They should sound hollow when tapped on the bottom. Remove from the oven and cool completely on a wire rack.

pain de campagne

Think of pain de campagne as sourdough's little brother. Sourdough is enjoying a huge renaissance in popularity; however, making it in the traditional fashion is a serious breadmaking event: a long, process in which a ferment is made without commercial yeast. The idea is that it attracts the natural, wild yeasts that are in the air all around us, allowing the dough to ferment very slowly, giving the bread its characteristicly robust flavor. In France the classic pain de campagne is used in a similar way to sourdough. You buy it to keep for a few days, as its flavor matures as it ages a little—and it lends itself beautifully to toasting and rubbing bruschetta-style with garlic. Leave the $1/2$ batch of rye dough in a bowl (covered with plastic wrap) to ferment for 4–6 hours, or overnight in the fridge and then brought back to room temperature before using.

Quantity:	2 loaves	
Preparation:	30 minutes	
Resting:	4–6 hours for the ferment	
	$2^1/2$ hours for the bread	
2nd Rising:	$1^1/4$ hours	
Baking:	30–35 minutes	

$1/2$ **Batch** rye dough (page 117) fermented

17$1/2$ ounces White bread flour (about $3^1/4$ cups)

3$1/2$ ounces Dark rye flour (about $3/4$ cup)

5g Fresh yeast (preferably) or a half-envelope active dry yeast ($3/4$ teaspoon)

$1/2$ ounce Salt (about 1 tablespoon fine-grain)

14 ounces Water (about 15 fl. oz. in measuring cup)

Flour for dusting

To make

• Use your scraper to scoop the ferment from its container into your bowl, all in one piece, and add the rest of your ingredients. Make the dough following the method on pages 22–25 and work it until you have a smooth dough which should be soft, supple, and elastic, and shouldn't feel sticky. Form it into a ball (page 25), and place in a lightly floured bowl, covered with a lintfree dishtowel, to rest for 1 hour.

• With the help of the rounded end of your scraper, turn the dough out onto a lightly floured counter and shape it into a ball again, put back in the bowl, cover, and let rest for a 1 hour.

• Repeat the above step, then cover, and let rest for 30 minutes. Using the rounded end of the scraper, turn the dough out onto a well floured counter and divide it into two pieces of about $1^1/4$ pounds each. Shape each into a ball. Lightly flour 2 wicker bread-rising baskets or line bowls with lintfree dishtowels, well dusted with flour, and put a ball of dough into each one, seam-side-down. Cover with another towel and let rise for about $1^1/4$ hours, or until they have nearly doubled in volume. Place the loaves, seam-side-down, on a peel or flat-edged cookie sheet, and cut a circle in the top of each loaf with a razor blade or sharp knife. Mist the inside of the preheated oven with a water spray. Slide the loaves onto the baking stone/tray and bake for 5 minutes. Turn down the heat to 425ºF (220°C) and bake for another 25–30 minutes until they are dark brown. The loaves should sound hollow if tapped on the bottom. Remove from the oven and cool on a wire rack.

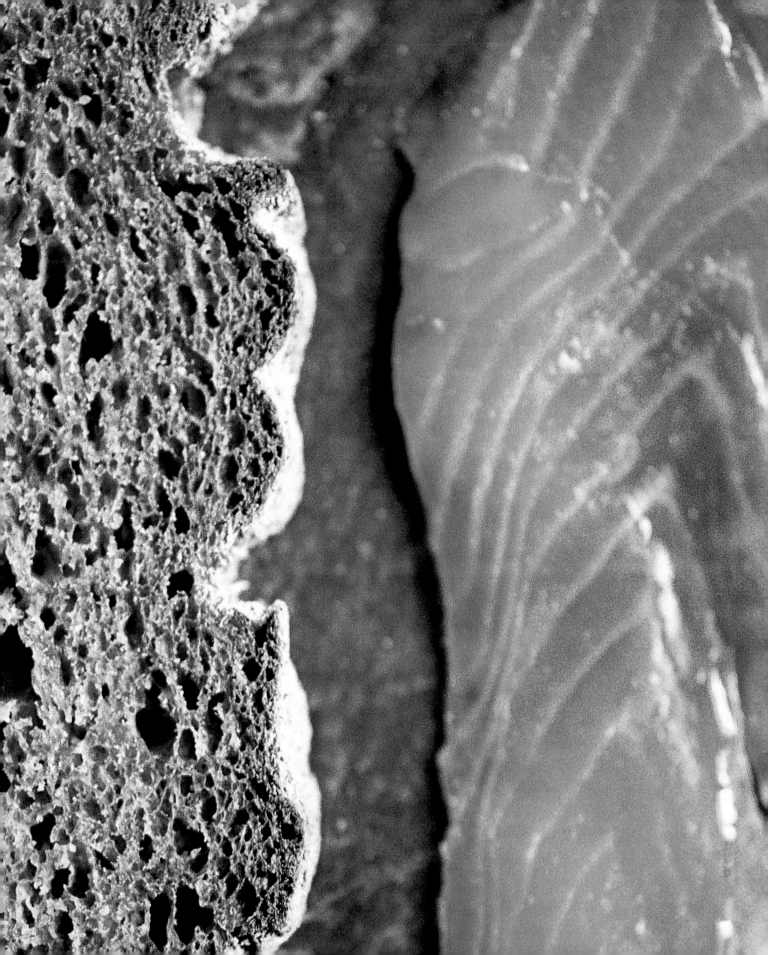

dark rye bread

This, again, is a slightly more complex loaf, boosted, with extra flavor from the "poolish" (page 114). While all bread should be allowed to cool before eating, dark rye bread, such as this one, can be especially indigestible if you eat it while still warm—let it cool down properly for several hours, before cutting into it.

Quantity:	2 loaves	**For the poolish:**		**7 ounces** Dark rye flour	
Preparation:	30 minutes	**6g** Fresh yeast		(about 1 1/2 cups)	
Resting:	3–5 hours for the poolish	**10 ounces** Tepid		**7 1/2 ounces** White bread	
	95 minutes for the dough	water (10 1/2 fl. oz. in		flour (about 1 1/2–1 2/3 cups)	
Proving:	1 hour	measuring cup)		**1/2 ounce** Salt (1 tablespoon)	
Baking:	45–50 minutes	**9 ounces** Dark rye		**4 ounces** Tepid water (about	
		flour (about 2 cups)		4 fl. oz. in measuring cup)	
				Flour for dusting	

To prepare

To make the poolish, whisk the yeast into the water until completely dissolved, then add the flour, and whisk to obtain a thick batter. Cover with a lintfree dishtowel and let it rest for at least 3 but no more than 5 hours. The poolish is ready to use when it forms a dome and then begins to flatten slightly. Once it reaches this point use it quickly, or it will start to collapse. Add the poolish to the rest of the ingredients and work/mix following the method on pages 22–25. Shape the dough into a ball (page 25) and place in to a lightly floured bowl, covered with a lintfree dishtowel, to rest for 45 minutes. Preheat the oven to 475°F (250°C).

To make

• With the help of the rounded end of your scraper, turn the dough out onto a lightly floured counter and reshape it into a ball, place back in the bowl, cover with a dishtowel and let rest for another 45 minutes.

• Using your scraper, turn the dough out onto your lightly floured counter and divide it into two equal pieces. Shape each into a ball and leave on the counter, covered with a lintfree dishtowel, to rest for another 5 minutes. Line two bread-rising baskets or bowls with well-floured lintfree dishtowels. Mold the loaves into tight balls and place them, seam-side down, on the towels. Cover with more towels and let rise for 1 hour or until they have nearly doubled in volume.

• Place the loaves on the peel or flat-edged cookie sheet, seam-side-down. Make four cuts in the top of each loaf, in each direction, to form a crisscross pattern. Open the preheated oven and mist with a water spray, then quickly slide the loaves onto the baking stone or tray. Bake them for 5 minutes, then turn down the heat to 400°F (200°C) for another 40–45 minutes. When the loaves are done they will look quite dark and sound hollow if tapped on the bottom. Remove and cool completely on a wire rack.

5. Sweet Dough

This dough is a cross between brioche and white bread and belongs to the family of "milk doughs". I love it because it isn't *too* sweet, yet it's sweet enough to carry the likes of chocolate, and although it is enriched with milk and butter, it isn't so rich that you couldn't use it, in its basic form, to make an excellent tuna sandwich, croque monsieur or serve it lightly toasted with foie gras.

For the recipes in this chapter, preheat the oven to 425°F (220°C) instead of 475°F (250°C).

9 ounces Whole milk (or 1 cup but it is more accurate to weigh it)

1/2 ounce Fresh yeast (preferably) or 1/4–oz. (7g) envelope active dry yeast

17 1/2 ounces White bread flour (about 3 3/4–4 cups)

2 ounces Unsalted butter (1/4 cup/1/2 stick) at room temperature

1 1/2 ounces Superfine sugar (about 3 tablespoons)

1/3 ounce Salt

2 Large eggs

To make the dough

• Pour the milk into a pan and warm gently until it is about body temperature — it should feel neither warm nor cold when you dip your finger into it. (You can use a microwave to do this if you prefer – about 1 1/2 minutes at full power.)

• To mix by hand, rub the yeast into the flour using your fingertips as if making a crumble. Rub in the butter, then add the sugar and salt, then the eggs and milk. Continue according to the method on pages 22–25.

bacon

orange &
mint loaf

pain
vienno

doughnut

sweet

fruited tea
loaf

scone

's
colate

cot &
ond

orange & mint loaf

I first made this when experimenting with a Marmalade Bread and Butter Pudding made with brioche and a dash of Grand Marnier. Instead of using brioche as a base, I wanted to try a more unusual bread that would really carry the flavor of the liqueur. From the starting point of orange, I tried infusing the dough with mint. The flavor was fantastic, and the bread kept well for several days, so I tried toasting it and serving it with a dish of fresh minted butter—and it was even better. I've also toasted it at breakfast time with scrambled eggs and crispy bacon. I love bread and butter pudding. However we do have something similar in France, which we used to do in the bakery to use up all the leftovers at the end of the day: croissants, pain au chocolat, you name it, everything would go into a big mixer with sultanas, crème anglaise, and some alcohol, until it became a thick paste, which we would bake for about 2 hours, cut up into portions and then dust with sugar. It tasted fantastic, and perhaps there is a little of its essence in this pudding, too.

Quantity:	2 large loaves	**1 Batch** Sweet dough (page 137)
Preparation:	20 minutes	**Bunch** of fresh mint
Resting:	2 hours	**Zest of 2** Large oranges
2nd Rising:	1½ hours	**1 tablespoon** Cointreau
Baking:	22–32 minutes	**1** Egg beaten with a pinch of salt for an egg wash
		Flour for dusting
		A little butter for greasing

To prepare

Infuse the milk for the dough with a bunch of mint by warming it through over low heat, then take the pan off the heat and leave it for 1 hour before straining. Make the sweet dough in the usual way using the mint-infused milk (page 137) and let it rest for 1 hour.

Mix the orange zest with the Cointreau. Lightly grease a cookie sheet with butter.

At the end of working the dough by hand/mixing in a mixer (page 24), add the orange zest, and incorporate it well. Form it into a ball (page 25), lightly flour the bowl, and put the dough back in to rest for 1 hour.

To make

• With the rounded end of your scraper, turn the dough out onto a very lightly floured counter and divide it into two equal portions. Mold each piece into a loaf shape (page 31) and place on the lightly greased cookie sheet. Brush the top of each loaf with egg wash. Let the egg wash dry for a moment, then cover the loaves with a lintfree dishtowel and let rise for 1½ hours, or until the dough has nearly doubled in volume and is springy when prodded. Brush again with egg wash. Using a pair of scissors held at 45° to the surface, make cuts along the top of each loaf. Put into the preheated oven, turn down the heat and bake at 410°F (210°C) for the first 2 minutes, then turn down to 400°F (200°C) and bake for another 20–30 minutes until the loaf is dark golden brown. Serve, toasted if you like, with mint butter.

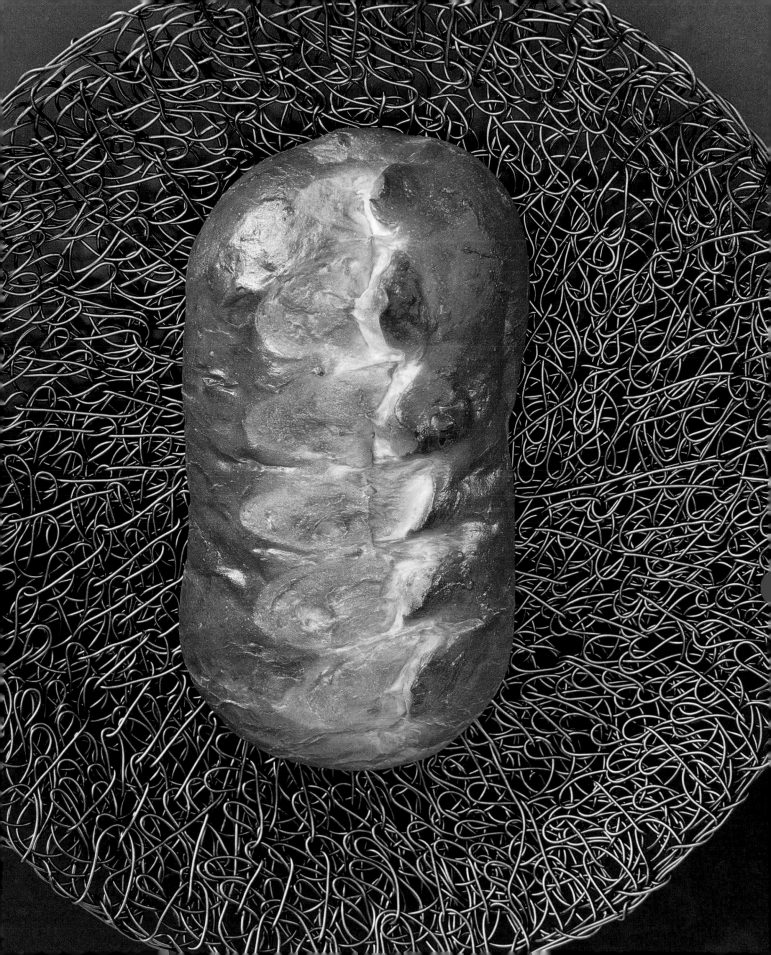

For the freezer: The loaf can happily be frozen, wrapped in freezer bags, and kept for 2–3 months.

mint butter

Put half a package of butter and a bunch of mint (leaves only) into a food processor and blitz until combined. Chill in a bowl in the fridge until required.

marmalade bread & butter pudding (6–8 people)

You can use the Orange and Mint Loaf for this—or alternatively buy some brioche. Whatever you choose, you will need two loaves.

Preheat the oven to 410°F (210°C) and soak 1 cup golden raisins in 4 tablespoons of Grand Marnier, while you make the crème anglaise. Do this by bringing 4 cups whole milk to a boil in a heavy pan along with a vanilla bean (split lengthwise and with the seeds scraped into the pan). Remove from the heat. In a bowl whisk 10 egg yolks and 150g caster sugar until they are a pale straw color and take on a mousse-like appearance.

Pour the milk into the egg mixture, whisking well as you do so. Return the mixture to the stove over a medium heat. Using a wooden spoon, stir continuously in a figure of 8 until it thickens enough to coat the back of a spoon. (To test, lift the spoon out of the crème and draw a line down the back of the spoon. If the line stays clean, it is cooked.) Strain immediately into a clean bowl and continue stirring for 1 minute.

Slice the orange and mint loaf or brioche—the slices need to be about 1/2-inch (1cm) thick. Spread with marmalade, then cut in half diagonally to form triangles. Strain the raisins, but don't throw away the Grand Marnier. Overlap the triangles (points up) in an ovenproof dish, making sure there are no gaps between the slices. Scatter the sultanas over them, pour the crème anglaise over the top, slowly, allowing time for the bread to absorb the liquid (there will probably be a good amount left, which you can keep back and serve with the pudding). Put in the preheated oven and cook for 20–30 minutes until golden brown on top.

To serve, warm the Grand Marnier in a small saucepan. Remove from the heat and light with a match. Pour it over the pudding and then sprinkle with a little sifted confectioners' sugar. Serve with crème fraîche, vanilla ice cream, or any remaining crème anglaise.

jack's chocolate buns

My son Jack loves pain aux raisins—and chocolate—so he badgered me to make him something that was a cross between the two. You should have seen Jack's face, lit up and covered in chocolate, when he bit into the first one I made. They are pretty gooey, so he is on rations: only one, for a treat!

Quantity:	24 buns
Preparation:	20 minutes
Resting:	45 minutes
2nd Rising:	$1^1/2$–$1^3/4$ hours
Baking:	12–15 minutes

1 Batch Sweet dough (page 137)

1 ounce Good-quality cocoa powder (about $^1/4$ cup)

7 ounces Chocolate chips, milk or dark, or a mixture of both, as you prefer (1 heaped cup)

2 Eggs beaten with a pinch of salt for an egg wash

Crème Patissière (page 158)

2 tablespoons cocoa powder

To prepare

Make the sweet dough following the method on page 137, but add the cocoa powder at the same time as the milk and egg, at the end of working the dough by hand or mixing in the mixer. Cover with a clean lintfree dishtowel and let rest for 45 minutes in a draft-free place.

Make the crème patissière following the recipe on page 158, but add 2 tablespoons cocoa powder to the milk. Pour into a dish to cool.

To make

• Using the rounded end of your scraper, transfer the dough to a lightly floured counter and, with a rolling pin, gently flatten it into a rough rectangle. Spread the chocolate crème patissière evenly over the dough and then sprinkle the chocolate chips on top. Starting with one of the longer edges, roll the dough up until it resembles a jelly roll. Using a sharp knife, cut the roll into $^3/4$-inch (2cm) slices and place them on their sides on a baking tray. Glaze with a little egg wash and let them rise for $1^1/2$–$1^3/4$ hours until the buns have roughly doubled in size.

• Glaze again and put into the preheated oven, turning the heat down to 350ºF (180ºC). Bake for 12–15 minutes. As the chocolate dough is quite dark, it can be difficult to tell when the buns are properly baked, and you need to take care not to underbake them—the best way to tell when they are ready is to lift one gently with a spatula, and check that it is firm underneath.

For the freezer: If you don't want to bake the buns all in one go, you can freeze some. When they are cut, just before rising, put them on a small tray in the freezer, and when they are hard, put them into a freezer bag. To use them, take them out, let them rise overnight and then bake in the same way.

doughnuts

These doughnuts come with a warning—don't even think of making them when you are on your own, as you may well end up eating the lot in one go—though if you have immense willpower, they will keep for a couple of days in the fridge as long as they haven't been dusted with sugar first. Personally I find that the moment I make a tray of them, they miraculously disappear, though mysteriously everyone says, "Nothing to do with me!"

Doughnuts ("beignets" in France) are of course a great classic, but I hate greasy ones, and I don't like ones with icing on them. I am locked into the memories of the beignets my grandmother used to make as a treat. I can still see the huge pan, with the risen dough bulging over the top (I would always be told off for prodding it) and I remember the wonderful smell and the anticipation as the first ones were fried, and then dusted in sugar or served with some jam or apple purée—which is still the only way I like to eat them.

Quantity:	30 doughnuts	
Preparation:	20 minutes	
Resting:	1 hour	
2nd Rising:	45 minutes	
Frying:	15 minutes	

1 Batch Sweet dough (page 137) rested for 1 hour

2 cups Good-quality peanut oil for frying

A little superfine sugar for coating the doughnuts

To fill the doughnuts (optional) either apple compote (page 158), raspberry jam or crème patissière (page 158)

Flour for dusting

Oil for greasing

To make

• With the help of the rounded end of your scraper, turn out the dough onto a lightly floured counter and form it into 30 tight balls (page 28) weighing about 1 ounce each. Lightly oil a baking tray and lightly dust it with flour. Arrange the doughnuts on top (seam-side-down), leaving sufficient space between them so that they will not touch as they rise. Cover the tray with a lintfree dishtowel and let rise until the doughnuts have nearly doubled in size—about 45 minutes.

• Pour the oil into an 8-inch (20cm) saucepan (any bigger and the oil won't be deep enough) and place over medium heat. When the oil is hot—allow about 15 minutes to reach the right heat—350°F (180°C), use a slotted spoon to lift the first doughnut and flip it over carefully into the oil. The doughnut should start sizzling right away. Add more until you fill the pan (I fry a maximum of five at a time). Fry for 30–45 seconds, until the doughnuts start to color and then turn them over and fry the other side for the same amount of time. Use the slotted spoon to remove them from the pan and drain on several sheets of paper towels. Let cool. For plain doughnuts, simply roll them in superfine sugar before serving. For filled doughnuts, spoon the filling of your choice into a pastry bag with a small nozzle and fill by inserting the nozzle into the doughnut at one side. How much filling you pipe in is up to you!

apricot & almond tart

You might wonder why I have included a tart in this book, but this is based on the sweet dough topped with mirabelles or gooseberries that my grandmother used to make. She would assemble the tart, then leave it for awhile, so that the dough rose up around the fruit and then, when she baked it, the juice would ooze out and into the dough. We would sprinkle sugar over the top before eating it, and it was just gorgeous. This is a slightly more elaborate version, with crème d'amande. I promise you, if you make up a big batch of sweet dough one day and use some for this tart and the rest to make doughnuts, you will be very, very popular!

Quantity:	2 tarts	**1 Batch** Sweet dough (page 137) rested for 1 hour
Preparation:	20 minutes	**10¹/₂ ounces** Crème d'amande—page 158
Resting:	95 minutes	(about 1¹/₃ cups)
2nd Rising:	45 minutes	**12–15** Fresh ripe apricots, or plums if you prefer
Baking:	20–25 minutes	**1** Egg beaten with a pinch of salt for an egg wash
		Flour for dusting
		A little confectioners' sugar or apricot jam, for serving

To make

• With the help of the rounded end of your scraper, turn out the dough onto a lightly floured counter, divide it in half, and shape each piece into a ball (page 25). Place in a floured bowl, cover with a lintfree dishtowel and let rest for 20 minutes.

• Grease two baking trays. Roll out each piece of dough to a circle of about 10–12 inches (25–30cm) diameter, place on the trays, and let rest for another 15 minutes.

• Quarter the apricots or plums. Spread the crème d'amande over the tart bases starting from the middle and stopping about 1 inch (2.5cm) from the edge. Arrange the fruit quarters on top, skin-side-down, packing them together as neatly as you can. Let the tarts rise for 45 minutes (when the edges will have risen to about double their original height).

• Brush egg wash evenly over the edges of the tart. Turn down the preheated oven to 400°F (200°C), and bake until the tips of the apricots or plums have browned (if the top colours too fast, turn down to 190°C) and the base is golden brown—about 20–25 minutes. Remove from the tray and cool on a wire rack. To serve, sprinkle a little confectioners' sugar over the tart, or glaze with clear, melted apricot jam.

Variation: Apple tart. Mix the almond cream with some apple compote (see page 158) and a drop of Calvados (or other apple brandy), and use peeled, sliced apples instead of apricots.

bacon "pastry slice"

You know when you have that craving for bacon that nothing else will satisfy? Well, being French, when I was an apprentice in the bakery, my cravings would be for a croque monsieur, made with lardons (our equivalent of bacon) and béchamel sauce (white sauce). We used to make an imitation by folding some bacon and béchamel into a piece of sweet dough and letting it rise, then baking it—wonderful!

Quantity:	6 slices
Preparation:	20 minutes
Resting:	1 hour
2nd Rising:	45 minutes
Baking:	15 minutes

1/2 Batch Sweet dough (page 137) rested for 1 hour

7 ounces Béchamel sauce (a scant cup)

1/2 16-oz. Package of Good-quality, preferably dry-cured, organic bacon

1 Medium egg beaten with a pinch of salt for an egg wash

3 1/2 ounces Grated Swiss cheese (about 1 cup)

To make

• With the help of the rounded end of your scraper, turn out the dough onto a lightly floured counter and form it into a ball (page 25). Roll the dough out to a thickness of about 1/4 inch (5mm) then cut it into 6 x 5-inch (12cm) squares. Spoon a tablespoon of béchamel in the center of one square, then fold two opposite corners together over it. Place a slice of bacon on top and then lift the whole slice onto a baking tray. Repeat with the other pastry slices. Cover with wax paper and then a lintfree dishtowel and let rise for 45 minutes.

• Glaze the exposed dough with the egg wash. Sprinkle some of the cheese on top. Turn the preheated oven down to 400°F (200°C) and bake them for about 15 minutes until they are a deep golden colour. Eat while they are still warm.

béchamel sauce

Melt 2 tablespoons unsalted butter over medium heat in a heavy pan. When it has all melted and is bubbling gently, add 2 1/2 tablespoons flour and whisk briskly off the heat until all of the butter has been absorbed and you have a putty-like paste that comes cleanly away from the pan. Add 2/3 cup whole milk, a little at a time, whisking continuously to ensure that no lumps form. Once all the milk has been added and you have a smooth sauce, cook over a low to medium heat until it starts to bubble. Cook for 1 more minute. Season with sea salt and freshly ground black pepper and a little ground nutmeg to taste. Let cool. This makes 7 ounces. For a richer sauce you can add 1/4–1/3 cup grated cheese (Cheddar or Gruyère work well) to the sauce while it is over the heat—make sure it melts completely.

fruited tea loaf

Traditional "tea bread" can sometimes be overly rich and heavy, but this one is nice and light—fantastic toasted, with fruit compote and fresh cream.

Quantity:	3 loaves
Preparation:	30 minutes
Resting:	65 minutes
2nd Rising:	1 1/2 hours
Baking:	25–30 minutes

1 Batch Sweet dough (page 137)

5 ounces Candied cherries, quartered (about 3/4 cup)

1/3 cup Candied peel or the grated zest of 2 large lemons and 2 large oranges

2 Large tablespoons Rum

4 ounces Slivered almonds (about 1 cup), plus some extra for topping

5 ounces Golden raisins (about 2/3 cup)

1 Medium egg beaten with a pinch of salt for an egg wash

To prepare

Grease 3 x 1-pound 8–8 1/2 inch (20–22cm long) loaf pans with butter.

Soak the cherries and peel or zest in the rum overnight.

Sprinkle the almonds on a baking tray and toast under the grill or in the hot oven, turning from time to time until they are golden brown. Let cool.

Mix all the fruit with the nuts and add the mixture to the dough towards the end of working by hand or mixing in the mixer, making sure it is evenly distributed. Shape the dough into a rough ball (page 25) and place in a lightly floured bowl. Let rest for 1 hour.

To make

• With the help of the rounded end of your scraper, turn the dough out onto a lightly floured counter and divide it into three equal pieces. Mold each into a rough ball and let rest for another 5 minutes.

• Mold each ball into a loaf (page 31) and place in the pans. Brush the tops with the egg wash. Cover the pans with a lintfree dishtowel and let rise for 1 1/2 hours or until the dough has nearly doubled in volume. Brush again with egg wash, and with a razor blade or sharp knife cut down the middle, and top with extra almonds.

• Bake in the preheated oven for 25–30 minutes until the crust is dark golden brown. Remove from the pans and check that the sides and underneath are golden. If not, put them back in for a few minutes (out of the pans). Let cool on a wire rack.

pain viennois

This dough is the bread you see in parts of France as an alternative to brioche. It's a recipe I teach regularly in my bread classes, and everyone finds it very simple to make. As kids we used to eat small baguettes made with this dough for breakfast, or at tea time—which we called "le quatre-heure". When we came home from school we would have them cut in half, with a bar of Poulain chocolate inside—these were the bars that every child ate, with the picture of a pony on the wrapper. You can also bake this in a tin and slice it for a croque monsieur.

Quantity:	5 baguettes or 15 rolls	**1 Batch** Sweet dough (page 137) rested for 1 hour
Preparation:	20 minutes	**1** Medium egg beaten with a pinch of salt for an egg wash
Resting:	1 hour	Flour for dusting
2nd Rising:	1 hour	
Baking:	8–12 minutes	

To make

With the help of the rounded end of your scraper, turn the dough out onto a lightly floured counter and divide it into five pieces for baguettes or fifteen pieces for rolls.

For the baguettes

• Flatten the pieces of dough with your hands into rough rectangles. Fold and roll according to the method on page 56. Place the baguettes on a tray with space between each, give them two coats of the egg wash, and then make a series of small deep cuts diagonally along the tops with a razor blade or sharp knife.

• Let rise for 1 hour then bake for 10–12 minutes in the preheated oven until the baguettes are dark golden brown.

For the rolls

• Form the pieces of dough into rolls (page 30).

• Place the rolls on a baking tray or trays, with space between each one.

• Glaze each roll with the egg wash, then with a knife or pair of scissors, make a cross in the tops, about 1/4-inch (5mm) deep.

• Let rise for 1 hour, then bake in the preheated oven for 8–10 minutes until the rolls are a dark golden brown.

scones

Everyone always asks me if I have a good recipe for scones. Well, I do. Ever since I first tried them when I came to Britain, they have been my favorite British speciality. We are still talking about dough, and this one has cream in it, which is a bit of a play on the tradition of cream scones. I also like to make my scones square, rather than round.

Quantity:	12–15 scones
Preparation:	20 minutes
Resting:	15 minutes
Baking:	20 minutes

5 ounces Salted butter (1 1/4 sticks or about 2/3 cup)

21 ounces All-purpose flour (about 4 1/4 –4 1/2 cups)

5 ounces Sugar (about 2/3 cup)

1/4 cup Baking powder

10 ounces Golden raisins (about 1 1/4 cups)

7 ounces Double cream (just under 1 cup)

4 ounces Milk (190g/ just under 1 cup)

2 Eggs, beaten with a pinch of salt for egg wash

To make

• Rub the butter into the flour in a mixing bowl. Add the sugar and baking powder. Add the raisins and mix the dough until they are evenly distributed.

• Add the cream and milk and mix with your scraper until all the ingredients are bound together. Lightly dust your counter with flour and turn the dough out onto it. Press down, then fold it in half, then press down again, fold again the opposite way, and then repeat, until you have a rough square. Flour the top and bottom of the dough, cover with a lintfree dishtowel, and let rest in a cool place for 15 minutes.

• Lightly flour the counter and then roll the dough out to a thickness of 1 inch (2.5–3cm). Brush off any excess flour. With a sharp knife, cut out the scones into squares—about 2 1/2 x 2 1/2 inches (6 x 6cm).

• Lay them on a baking tray, making sure that the scones are not too close together. Roll out any remaining scraps of dough and cut some more scones until you have used all of the dough.

• Glaze the scones with the egg wash. Wait for 2 minutes, then glaze again.

• Turn down the heat in the preheated oven to 400°F (200°C) and bake the scones for around 20 minutes until they are well raised, and the top and underside is golden brown.

additional recipes

apple compote

Peel, core and quarter 2 large cooking apples. Melt a large knob of butter in a pan on the stove and add 1 teaspoon of sugar and a pinch of cinnamon. Add the apples and toss until well coated with butter. Cook for 1 minute or so, then reduce the heat, add a tablespoon of Calvados or brandy (if you like) and stir well. Cover the pan and leave over a low heat for 10–15 minutes, or until the apples are soft. Remove from heat and cool for a few minutes, then, using a hand blender, blitz until smooth and leave to cool completely.

crème patissière

In a bowl whisk together 6 egg yolks, 3 ounces caster sugar and 2 ounces sifted flour. Put another 3 ounces sugar into a pan with 2 cups full-fat milk and a vanilla pod (split lengthwise and seeds scraped in). Place over a low heat. Leave until the first bubble appears, then remove from the heat. Whisk $1/3$ of the milk into the egg mixture, then add the remaining $2/3$ of the milk and stir again. Pour back into the pan and put back on the heat. Bring to a boil and simmer for a couple of minutes, stirring constantly to ensure that the cream does not burn on the bottom of the pan Pour into a dish to cool. Sprinkle a little icing sugar or flakes of butter on top to prevent a skin forming.

crème d'amande

Beat $1 1/4$ sticks butter (at room temperature) and $4 1/2$ ounces caster sugar by hand, or mix in a food processor with a paddle, until pale and fluffy. Add $4 1/2$ ounces ground almonds and mix again. Add 1 ounce plain flour and continue to mix, finally adding 2 eggs, one at a time, along with 2 large tablespoons of rum (if you like), mixing well between each addition, until the mixture is light in consistency. Use immediately or store in an airtight container in the fridge for up to a week.

suppliers

BACON
Diamond Organics www.dimaondorganics.com
888 674 2642

BAKING EQUIPMENT
Williams Sonoma www.williams-sonoma.com
877 812 6235
The Bertinet Kitchen www.thebertinetkitchen.com

CIDER
Stone Ridge Orchard
www.stoneridgeorchard.com
845 687 2587

DELIS
Dean & Deluca www.deandeluca.com

FLOUR
King Arthur Flour www.kingarthurflour.com
802 649 3881

OILS
Any good extra virgin olive oil will do but I particularly like Belazu www.belazu.com
The avocado oil I use is made by Olivado Gourmet Foods www.olivado.com

FRESH YEAST
All bakeries or supermarket in-store bakeries should be able to sell you some but you will need to ask. Many delis or health food stores may also stock it. Again, if they don't, ask because they may be able to order it from their bakery supplier.
Red Star Yeast
www.redstaryeast.com
877 677 7000

index